Renaissance Papers
2023

Renaissance Papers 2023

Editors
Lisandra Estevez and Jim Pearce

Editorial Assistant
Vergil Demery

Published for
THE SOUTHEASTERN RENAISSANCE CONFERENCE
by
Camden House
Rochester, New York

The Southeastern Renaissance Conference

2023 Officers

President: Ward Risvold, Georgia College & State University
Vice-President: Jonathan Shelley, St. John Fisher University
Secretary: Jesse Russell, Georgia Southwestern State University
Treasurer: Eric Dunnum, Campbell University

Renaissance Papers, 2023

Copyright © 2024
The Southeastern Renaissance Conference

All rights reserved
Library of Congress Catalog Number A 55-3551

SSN: 0584-4207
ISBN-13: 978-1-64014-187-2

Published by:

Camden House
An imprint of Boydell & Brewer, Inc.
668 Mt. Hope Avenue, Rochester, NY 14620-2731, USA
and of Boydell & Brewer Ltd.
P.O. Box 9, Woodbridge, Suffolk IP12 3DF, UK
www.boydellandbrewer.com

CONTENTS

Spenser's Secret Teaching: Socratic Irony, Ritual Platonism, and the Unveiling of *The Faerie Queene*
JESSE RUSSELL 1

Edwardian Evangelicalism in Queen Elizabeth's Reign: William Baldwin's *Funeralles of King Edward The Sixt*
SCOTT LUCAS 15

The Religious Dynamics of Robert Herrick's "Rex Tragicus"
PAUL J. STAPLETON 27

Rewriting the Psalmist: Form and Gender in *A Meditation of a Penitent Sinner*
MARY RUTH ROBINSON 39

Renaissance Utopia as Deliberative Monologue: Andrzej Frycz Modrzewski and Thomas More
VÁCLAV ZHENG 55

Alonso Berruguete's Workshop and the Place
of Polychrome Sculpture in the Hierarchy of
Arts in Spain
    Ilenia Colón Mendoza   71

From Scripture to Spectacle: Fiction, Religion,
and the Visual in Maarten van Heemskerk's
Ecce Homo (1544)
    Sunmin Cha   85

In the Wake of the Emperor: The Depiction
of Don Carlos of Austria as *Miles Christi* in
Juan de Angulo's Illustrated Manuscript
    Gerardo Rappazzo Amura   101

Inventing John Donne: Temptations of
the Biographer
    John N. Wall   123

Renaissance Papers

A Selection of Papers
Submitted to the
Eightieth Annual Meeting
September 29–30, 2023
University of North Carolina, Chapel Hill
Chapel Hill, North Carolina

Spenser's Secret Teaching: Socratic Irony, Ritual Platonism, and the Unveiling of *The Faerie Queene*

Jesse Russell

FOLLOWING the 2009 release of *Spenser Studies'* special issue, "Spenser and Platonism," Spenser scholars have embraced the notion that the Renaissance English poet, Edmund Spenser, very likely was well versed in the texts of the Greek philosopher Plato as well as his Italian Renaissance disciple, Marsilio Ficino (1433–99). This recent critical discussion has continued and has, for the time being, finalized an earlier debate between scholars such as Robert Ellrodt,[1] on one hand, who argued that Spenser derived much of his knowledge of Platonism from works derived from antiquity and medieval Christianity, and C. S. Lewis[2] and Carol Kaske,[3] on the other, who argued for a more intimate familiarity

---

1 Robert Ellrodt famously dismissed the presence of any use of Platonic or "Neoplatonic" texts outside of Medieval Christian works by Spenser until his later career in *Neoplatonism in the Poetry of Spenser* (Geneva: Librairie Droz, 1960).

2 C. S. Lewis presents his view of Spenser as a definitively Protestant Platonist, whose Platonism is always subordinate to his Protestantism in works such as *The Allegory of Love: A Study in Medieval Tradition* (Cambridge: Cambridge Univ. Press, 2016), his *English Literature in the Sixteenth Century, Excluding Drama* (Oxford: Oxford Univ. Press, 1954), and his chapter "Neoplatonism in the Poetry of Edmund Spenser," in *Studies in Medieval and Renaissance Literature* (Cambridge: Cambridge Univ. Press, 1966).

3 Carol Kaske revived the "Ellrodt Debate" with "Neoplatonism in Spenser once More," *Religion and Literature* 32, no. 2 (2000): 157–69.

between Spenser and the works of Plato and Plato's Renaissance disciples. The discussion of the presence of Plato in Spenser, while largely focused on metaphysics and aesthetics, also has included, fittingly, *sub rosa* treatment of Spenser's interest in the writings of Platonists who explored what has been called Hermeticism, "Neo-Platonic magic," and "ritual Platonism."

The last half of the twentieth century saw the surge (and then slow demise) of Warburg School writers such as Francis Yates[4], David French[5], Douglas Brooks Davies,[6] and others who argued that Edmund Spenser was deeply involved with the occult philosophy of the Renaissance.[7] Acknowledging that Spenser apparently had some significant knowledge of magic, scholars such as

---

Ellrodt, in turn, moderated his views and seemed to accept many of Kaske's arguments in "Fundamental Modes of Thought, Imagination, and Sensibility in the Poetry of Spenser," *Spenser Studies* 20 (2005): 1–21.

4   Yates's watershed work is *Giordano Bruno and the Hermetic Tradition* (Chicago: Univ. of Chicago Press, 1964). Yates followed *Giordano Bruno* with the similarly successful and groundbreaking *The Art of Memory* (New York: Routledge, 1966). In *Theatre of the World* (Chicago: Univ. of Chicago Press, 1969) and *The Occult Philosophy in the Elizabethan Age* (New York: Routledge, 1979), as well as in her compendium of earlier essays, *Astraea: The Imperial Theme in the Sixteenth Century* (New York: Routledge, 1975), Yates further explores the important place that occultism, magic, and esoterica occupied in Renaissance culture.

5   Peter French, *John Dee: The World of an Elizabethan Magus* (London: Routledge, 1972).

6   Douglas Brooks-Davies, *The Mercurian Monarch: Magical Politics from Spenser to Pope* (Manchester: Manchester Univ. Press, 1982).

7   Several twentieth-century scholars of magic in the Renaissance have all too briefly treated Spenser's interest in the occult. See Katharine Mary Briggs, *Pale Hecate's Team: An Examination of the Beliefs on Witchcraft and Magic among Shakespeare's Contemporaries and His Immediate Successors* (London: Routledge, 1962), 75–76; John S. Mebane, *Renaissance Magic and the Return of the Golden Age: The Occult Tradition and Marlowe, Jonson, and Shakespeare* (Lincoln: Univ. of Nebraska Press, 1992), 139; John Mulryan, "The Occult Tradition in English Renaissance Literature," *The Bucknell Review* 20, no. 3 (1972): 53–72; Wayne Shumaker, *The Occult Sciences in the Renaissance* (Berkeley: Univ. of California Press, 1972), 240; Kenneth Gross, *Spenserian Poetics: Idolatry, Iconoclasm, and Magic* (Ithaca, NY: Cornell Univ. Press, 1986).

A. Bartlett Giamatti[8] and Patrick Cheney[9] tamed the "Yates thesis," arguing that Spenser employed magical concepts in the framing of the power of his poetics. In the twenty-first century scholars such as Jon Quitslund,[10] Genevieve Guenther,[11] and Jesse Russell[12] have revived elements of the "Yates thesis," arguing that the presence of magical concepts in Spenser's poetry is significant.

Whether or not Spenser himself took magic seriously during some portion of his life is a curious question, but it is not a question that needs to be answered in this essay. It is quite clear that Spenser had knowledge of Platonic ideas and access to Platonic works and, at the same time, it is very likely that he uses concepts and language from ritual or magical Platonism to frame his works—especially his *Faerie Queene*. One of the key concepts from ritual Platonism that Spenser uses is the notion of the power of the enlightened individual—whether as philosopher, mystic, poet, or even magus—to peer behind the veil of ignorance and have access to hidden Divine truths. In *The Faerie Queene* Edmund Spenser presents himself as what Jon Quitslund has called a "poet magus" who has access to a hidden teaching or experience of Divine things. However, as *The Faerie Queene* proceeds into the "Two Cantos of Mutabilitie" appended to the 1609 edition, Spenser appears to lose faith in the

---

8 A. Bartlett Giamatti, *The Earthly Paradise and the Renaissance Epic* (Princeton, NJ: Princeton Univ. Press, 1969).

9 Patrick Gerard Cheney, "'Secret Power Unseene'": Good Magic in Spenser's Legend of Britomart," *Studies in Philology* 85, no. 1 (1988): 1–28 as well as Cheney's "'And Doubted Her to Deeme and Earthly Wight': Male Neoplatonic 'Magic' and the Problem of Female Identity in Spenser's Allegory of the Two Florimells," *Studies in Philology* 86, no. 3 (1989): 310–40.

10 Jon Quitslund, *Spenser's Supreme Fiction: Platonic Natural History and "The Faerie Queene"* (Toronto: Univ. of Toronto Press, 2001).

11 See Guenther's "Spenser's Magic, or Instrumental Aesthetics in the 1590 *Faerie Queene*," *ELR* 36, no. 2 (2006): 194–226 as well as her book length treatment *Magical Imaginations: Instrumental Aesthetics in the Renaissance* (Toronto: Univ. of Toronto Press, 2012).

12 Jesse Russell, "Spenser's Ancient Hope: The Rise and Fall of the Dream of the Golden Age in *The Faerie Queene*," *Explorations in Renaissance Culture* 44, no. 1 (2018): 73–103.

poet's ability to peer behind the veil of knowledge and retreats into quiet Christian humility.

Veiling and Unveiling in *The Faerie Queene*

While there are lots of veils in *The Faerie Queene* that serve the simple function of covering (mostly female characters) in the poem, there are veils, which appear to serve as allegories or representatives of hidden knowledge and experience. One of the most critical characters in Book I, Una, who, while being a major figure in the plot of the poem, also serves as an allegory for the one true English Church, hides her ivory face "Vnder a vele, that wimpled was full low . . ." (I.i.4). This veil serves as a cover for her as a modest Christian royal who is "pure" and "innocent" (I.i.5), but it also accentuates her sacred character as an allegorical representation of true religion as well as ". . . Truth in its philosophical aspects."[13] Later, in canto vi of Book I, in a deeply symbolic violation of both a woman and the divine truth she represents, the pagan Sansloy rips the veil from Una's face from which "her beautie shyne[s], as brightest skye . . ." (I.vi.4). Spenser further accentuates the divine beauty of Una when he describes her as divine, angelic, and illuminating in Book I, Canto iii. Resting in a "secret shadow," Una removes her veil, her "fillet" and "stole" and unveils her beautiful "angels face," which "As the great eye of heauen shyned bright, / and made a sunshine in the shady place . . ." (I.iii.4). Spenser further states that no "mortall eye" has ever beheld "such heauenly grace" (I.iii.4). Once again, the veil of Una hides divine beauty and grace, not simply a pretty face. Una again unveils in Book I, Canto xii, tossing away her "mournefull stole" and "sad wimple" with which she hides her "heauenly beautie" (I.xii.22). As he will in his description of Elizabeth's own beauty as well as with other sources of sublime and heavenly experience in *The Faerie Queene*, Spenser illustrates how Una's heavenly beauty is so great as to defy his ability to describe: "The blazing brightness of her beauties beame, / And glorious light of her sunshyny face . . ." is so great that his "ragged rimes all too rude and

---

13 Douglas Brooks-Davies, "Una," in A. C. Hamilton et al., eds. *The Spenser Encyclopedia* (Toronto: Univ. of Toronto Press, 1990), 705.

bace" to depict her "heauenly lineaments ..." (I.xii.23). Even Redcrosse himself, "her own deare loued knight," wonders at the "celestiall sight..." (I.xii.23). The veil that hid Una hid a divine and holy beauty to which only a few, including Spenser and his privileged reader, have access. As we will see, this image of veiled beauty is used by Spenser to describe Elizabeth as well as the divine beauty to which Spenser as poet magus has access—interestingly, Una herself, as Douglas Brooks-Davies argues, is "a cult name for Elizabeth, the one Supreme Governor of the Church of England ..."[14] The beauty hidden by Una's veil is thus a divine and holy beauty connected with the beauty of true religion and the ultimate divine beauty of God.

Una is not the only figure in the poem whose beauty and divine radiance are hidden behind a veil. In canto v of Book IV, Cambell introduces his wife, Cambina, who is "couered with a veale" (IV.v.10). When this veil is withdrawn, "most perfect hew / and passing beauty did efsoones reueale ..." (IV.v.10). Cambina herself is later described as a "Ladie passing faire / An bright, that seemed borne of Angels brood, / And with her beautie bountie did compare, / Whether of them in her should haue the greater share" (IV. iii.39). Cambina is, like Una herself (as well as Mutability), a figure associated with divine and royal power.

In Book I, a similar sort of veil hides the divine radiance of Arthur's diamond shield, which, as Douglas Brooks-Davies notes, is linked with the face of Una in its solar radiance.[15] This diamond shield is linked with solar and lunar power and even, as Spenser explicitly states, with magic: "For so exceeding shone his glistering ray, / That *Phoebus* golden face it did attaint, / As when a cloud his beames doth ouer-lay / And siluer *Cynthia* wexed pale and faynt, / As when her face is staynd with magicke arts constraint" (I.vii.34). This shield formed by Merlin is resistant to magic arts and can even turn men to stones and stones to dust, "and dust to nought at all" (I.vii.35). Interestingly, this shield is also covered with a veil that hides its divine and magic power. When Arthur is knocked down by the giant Orgoglio in canto viii of the first book, the "vele" covering the shield falls and out shines "The light wereof, that heuens light did pas, / Such blazing brightnesse through the ayer threw, /

---

14 Ibid., 705.
15 Ibid., 705.

That eye mote not the same endure to vew" (I.viii.19). Again, a veil is used to cover a spiritual brightness. This shield is a magic object made by Merlin himself. In Book V, Canto viii, Arthur removes the shield from the veil, "which did his powerfull light empeach ..." (V.viii.37). Arthur reveals the shield to a group of horses pulling the Souldan and "Like lightening flash, that hath the gazer burned, / So did the sight thereof their sense dismay, / That backe againe vpon themselues they turned ..." (V.viii.38). Arthur's shield like the countenance of Una (and, to lesser degree, Cambina) was veiled to hide its radiant magic power.

As a further example of a veiled divinity in the poem, there is the idol in Venus's temple, which "in shape and beautie did excel" all others is "couered with a slender veile afore ..." (IV.x.40). We learn that the veiling of this statue is due to its hermaphroditic character:

> The cause why she was couered with a vele,
> Was hard to know, for that her Priests the same
> From peoples knowledge labour'd to concele.
> But sooth it was not sure womanish shame,
> Nor any blemish, which the worke of mote blame;
> But for, they say, she hath both kinds in one,
> Both male and female, both vnder one name:
> She syre and mother is her selfe alone,
> Begets and eke conceiues, he needeth other none. (IV.x.41)

Venus's idol is a seemingly monstrous figure, but it also serves as an image of perfect beauty and power. Commenting on this passage, Edgar Wind writes that the statue is part of a tradition of monstrous images of God's power found in the Biblical texts such as Ezekiel and the Book of the Apocalypse that suggest that "when God appears to His prophets, His supernatural powers are displayed through monstrous apparitions."[16] Moreover, in the Platonic tradition, Wind argues, "the first and original man was androgynous" and "the divisions into male and female belonged to a latter and lower state of creation; and that, when all created things return to their maker, the unfolded and divided state of man will be re-enfolded

---

16 Edgar Wind, *Pagan Mysteries in the Renaissance* (New Haven, CT: Yale Univ. Press, 1958), 173.

in the divine essence."[17] Whether or not Spenser was drawing from this Platonic tradition in his framing of Venus's statue's hermaphroditism, the statue nonetheless is veiled, and as such is a source of divine and hidden power.

Finally, False Florimell, the deceptive product of witchcraft, also is "[c]overed from peoples gazement with a vele" (V.iii.17). When the people discover it is her, they are amazed and "stupefide (V.iii.17), for "So feeble skill of perfect things the vulgar has" (V.iii.17). This language is highly redolent of the text of Renaissance Platonists who expressed interest in ritual Platonism. Spenser even seems to link False Florimell with the (veiled) divine, solar radiance of Una, Cambina and Arthur's shield. Spenser writes that even true Florimell's lover, Marinell, is confused at the sight of False Florimell who appears like a deceptive second sun in the sky, creating a "strange prodigous sight ..." (V.iii.19). With strange figures like Venus's statue and False Florimell even the semblance of beauty must be veiled and hidden from the profane viewer. This concept of veiling language from the profane in Spenser's *Faerie Queene* is drawn, either directly or indirectly, from the texts of ritual Platonists and magi of the Renaissance.

Socratic Irony and Veiling in Ritual Platonism

Dilwyn Knox treats the Medieval and Renaissance conceptions of irony in his 1989 *Ironia: Medieval and Renaissance Ideas on Irony*. In *Ironia*, Knox argues that *ironia* "as medieval and Renaissance authors themselves explained, was a figure or trope, that is, a means of establishing discourse."[18] Socratic irony, in particular was identified in the Renaissance by figures such as Erasmus as being a veil of humility for Socrates's wisdom.[19] In addition to self-deprecation, Renaissance thinkers ascribed concealment as another characteristic

---

17 Ibid., 173.
18 Dilwyn Knox, *Ironia: Medieval and Renaissance Ideas on Irony* (Leiden: Brill, 1989), 9.
19 Ibid., 112.

of Socratic irony.[20] It is this concept of concealment or veiling the truth that is especially germane to our discussion.

Wind treats this concept of veiling in his 1958 work, *Pagan Mysteries in the Renaissance*. Wind traces the language of ritual Platonism employed by Renaissance thinkers to Socratic or Platonic irony, specially to Plato's famous Seventh letter in which Plato argued that his philosophy offered what had previously been offered to the initiate in the Eleusinian mysteries, including "the cleansing of the soul, the welcoming of death, the power to enter into communion with the Beyond, the ability to 'rage correctly'...," which could be obtained "by rational exercise, by a training in the art of dialectic, whose aim it was to purge the soul of error."[21] Wind further points to a passage in *The Republic* in which Plato states that the Muses communicate to mock humans and ironically "in solemn mockery ... play and jest with us as if we were children, and to address us in a lofty tragic vein, making believe to be in earnest?"[22] Wind thus argues that the Platonic tradition, "with a note of irony, but then thoroughly systematized by Plotinus," undertakes "the adoption of a ritual terminology to assist and incite the exercise of intelligence ..."[23] However, Wind brilliantly argues that Plato's tearing of mysticism away from ritual ultimately failed, and "the adoption of ritual terminology to assist and incite the exercise of intelligence proved exceedingly useful as a fiction, but ended, as such fictions are likely to do, by betraying the late Platonists into a revival of magic."[24] Later Platonists, who were studied and translated by Renaissance Platonists like Ficino such as Iamblichus (AD 245–325) and Proclus (AD 412–85), revived a host of ritual magical practices that had been shunned by Plato and his immediate followers.

These ideas were transmitted in various forms to Renaissance Christian Platonists such as Ficino who often employed ironic and veiled language to avoid ecclesiastical scrutiny of his ideas in works such as *Theologia Platonica* (1482) as well as in letters to figures such

---

20 Ibid., 114.
21 Wind, *Pagan Mysteries in the Renaissance*, 14.
22 Plato, *Republic*, 545–47, qtd. in Wind, *Pagan Mysteries in the Renaissance*, 15.
23 Wind, *Pagan Mysteries in the Renaissance*, 15.
24 Ibid., 15.

as Braccio Martelli and in Ficino's many commentaries on pagan works; as Carol Kaske and John Clark argue in their introduction to Ficino's 1489 *De vita libri tres*, "it appears that the commentary as a literary form allowed him to say things which he believed but which he could not as a Christian, and latterly as a priest, have said *in propria persona*."[25] In his treatment of Plato's *Parmenides*, Ficino writes how both numbers and poetic figures are "'veils' that hid the nakedness of truth from the vulgar gaze, or as a 'rind' that protects its sweet kernel"; these figures could also serve as "intellectual baits that will lure the subtle into the paths of righteous inquiry."[26] In his preface to his 1471 translation of the *Corpus Hermeticum*, Ficino further explains how this veiling was common among the vessels of the *prisca theologia* who "covered all the sacred mysteries of divine things with poetic veils..."[27] Finally, in his Commentary on Plotinus's *Enneads* (1492), after praising the Platonic philosopher for unveiling philosophy, Ficino argues that Plotinus had "been inspired by heaven to penetrate the secrets of the ancients" without granting access to profane readers.[28] In Ficino, there is a clear understanding that a wise person has access to peer behind the veil of knowledge to uncover divine truth, but this truth must not be shared with the profane.

Ficino's erstwhile disciple, Pico della Mirandola (1463–94) likewise wrote of his own work as being "intelligible only to a few, for it is filled with many mysteries from the secret philosophy of the ancients."[29] Mirandola further explains in his commentary on the *Canzona d'amore* that "divine subjects and secret Mysteries must not be rashly divulged... That is why the Egyptians had sculptures of sphinxes in all their temples, to indicate that divine knowledge, if committed to writing at all, must be covered with enigmatic veils

---

25 Marsilio Ficino, *Three Books on Life* translated by Carol V. Kaske and John R. Clarke (Binghamton, NY: MRTS, 1989), 64–65.
26 Michael J. B. Allen, *Icastes: Marsilio Ficino's Interpretation of Plato's Sophist* (Berkeley: Univ. of California Press, 1989), 76.
27 Quoted in Paul Oskar Kristeller, *The Philosophy of Marsilio Ficino*, trans. Virginia Conant (New York: Columbia Univ. Press, 1960), 26.
28 Allen, *Icastes*, 51.
29 Quoted in Wind, *Pagan Mysteries in the Renaissance*, 19.

and poetic dissimulation ..."[30] The philosopher must use ironic and elliptical writing to convey his own ideas. Both Ficino and Pico wrote works that treated magic from a theoretical perspective. However, even those who were involved in ritual magic, wrote in such a way as to veil their true intent.

The notorious occultist Cornelius Agrippa (1486–1535) writes in his *De Occulta Philosophia libri III* (1531–33) that he has "writ many things, rather narratively than affirmatively" in order that he can convey "this art in such a manner, that it may not be hid from the prudent and intelligent, and yet may not admit the wicked and incredulous to the mysteries of these secrets."[31] Agrippa also writes of his veiling in Book 3 of *De Occulta Philosophia*, hiding the "mysteries of these secrets" from "wicked and incredulous men."[32] Agrippa's address to the reader: "Judicious Reader!" at the beginning of *De occulta Philosophia*, further states, "There is the outside, and the inside of philosophy; but the former without the latter is but an empty flourish; yet with this alone most are satisfied."[33] As with Ficino and Pico, from whom Agrippa drew, the wise person, in Agrippa's thought, has access to a veiled and hidden knowledge that must be kept from the profane. Scholars have demonstrated Spenser's access to Ficino's texts,[34] yet the writings of Agrippa as well could have been available to Tudor and Stuart poets. Although born in the city of Cologne, Germany in 1486, Agrippa traveled widely throughout Europe, visiting England in 1510. During his visit, Agrippa, according to a legend handed down by Thomas Nashe and, later, Sir Walter Scott, allowed The Earl of Surrey, Henry Howard, to see a deceased beloved in a magic mirror.[35] The German magus

---

30 Wind, *Pagan Mysteries in the Renaissance*, 24.
31 Cornelius Agrippa, *Three Books of Occult Philosophy*, trans. James Freake, ed. Donald Tyson (Woodbury, MN: Llewellyn Publications, 2009), 667.
32 Ibid., 667.
33 Ibid., lxi.
34 See Valery Rees, "Ficinian Ideas in the Poetry of Edmund Spenser," *Spenser Studies* 24 (2009): 73–134.
35 Charles Nauert, *Agrippa and the Crisis of Renaissance Thought* (Champaign: Univ. of Illinois Press, 1964), 328.

further left an intellectual footprint on England that would influence Spenser's contemporary John Dee.[36]

Peering behind the Veil: Spenser as Poet Magus

Spenser seems to refer to this image of himself as a celestial thief in his Letter to Sir Walter Raleigh appended to the 1590 edition of the poem. Presenting the letter as a key to understanding his allegorical work, Spenser comments on the ambiguity of allegory or "how doubtfully all Allegories may be construed ..." and refers to his work as a "continued Allegory, or dark conceit."[37] While most critics rightly have acknowledged that Spenser is simply saying that he is using enigmatic, allegorical methods to convey formal truths, others have acknowledged that the expression "dark conceit"[38] may contain a subtle message that the allegory contains a deeper meaning veiled from the pedestrian reader, and Spenser is a poet magus who has obtained access to this hidden knowledge.[39]

In order to affect this fashioning of the reader, Spenser as poet magus must have access behind the veil, an ability that Spenser claims to have in the proems to *The Faerie Queene*'s books. In the proem to Book I, Spenser tells the reader that he will "sing of Knights and Ladies gentle deeds," whose "praises" had "slept in silence long ..." (I.i.1). The language here indicates that Spenser is reviving a forgotten lore or tradition that will be revealed to him by a "holy virgin" muse who will unveil from her "euerlasting

---

36 French, *John Dee*, 1.

37 I draw my quotes from A. C. Hamilton's edition of *The Faerie Queene* (New York: Routledge, 2013), 714.

38 John Mulryan argues that the phrase "darke conceit" should be read with Una's veil as well as the veil of Venus in Book IV and the veil of Nature in the "Two Cantos of Mutabilitie" as signs of an occult "learned obscurity" woven throughout *The Faerie Queene*. Mulryan, "The Occult Tradition in English Renaissance Literature," 64.

39 Presenting a representative "tame," explanation of this phrase, Lewis argues that the Spenser's use of the phrase "continued allegory or dark conceit" is an indication that while he was, "borrowing from the form of the Italian epic," he was continuing "the medieval impulse" of moral allegory. Lewis, *The Allegory of Love*, 372.

scryne" the "antique rolles, which there lye hidden still, / Of Faerie knights and fairest *Tanaquill* . . ." (I.i.2). The muse here, perhaps, as A. C. Hamilton suggests, Clio, the muse of history, will reveal to Spenser a hidden history of Britain. But this hidden history is simultaneously a mythic world that contains both an idealization of the British as Faerie knights and Queen Elizabeth as fairest *Tanaquill* as well as sobering realistic depictions of them. The notion that Spenser is gaining access to hidden memories and ancient history is continued in the proem to Book II in which Spenser tells his "most mighty Soueraine" that some may accuse him of creating a fictitious world or "painted forgery" sprung from his "ydle braine" (II.Proem.1). Rather, Spenser assures Elizabeth and the other readers, the English poet will produce a "matter of iust memory" (II. Proem.1), for Spenser has with the aid of his muse access to a hidden realm to which other, more pedestrian poets and seers do not have access. Spenser lets us know that this realm to which he has access is unknown to "those that breatheth liuing aire" (II.Proem.1).

In addition to his Letter to Raleigh, Spenser appears to refer to himself as a poet magus with access to a world behind the veil hiding divine knowledge throughout the proems that stand as hinges to the various books of *The Faerie Queene*. In the proem of Book II, Spenser presents another charmed key to reading his poem, suggesting that the poet's work is not simply an allegory of virtues, but is an enigmatic and revelatory work drawn from Spenser's own apparently mystical poetic intuition. Preparing the reader for the lengthy genealogies in Canto x, in Book II's proem, Spenser directly addresses Elizabeth, paradoxically telling her that even though he is *not* going to "show" her the "happy land of Faery," he is going to "vouch antiquities, which no body, can know" (II.Proem.1).[40] Thus, maintaining the enigmatic tone of the Letter to Raleigh, Spenser says that in his "darke conceit" he is both going to reveal the antiquities of Faerie Land and not reveal them. Regardless of Spenser's ultimate meaning, he has access to a hidden world of knowledge and experience privileged to him as a poet with Promethean-like powers of intuition.

---

40 Quitslund specifically points to the Proems of Books II and VI as "reference points for the terms in which Spenser conceived his relationship to the world of his book." Quitslund, *Spenser's Supreme Fiction*, 73.

He continues, explaining that these antiquities "haue from wisest ages hidden beene" and "later times things more vnknowne shall show" (II.Proem.3). Consequently, Spenser, perhaps both puckishly and sincerely, reveals that there is a hidden teaching that he will present to Elizabeth in Book II, which will be manifested in some obscure way. If we look at this passage with the description of *The Faerie Queene* as a "darke conceit" in the Letter to Raleigh, it seems that Spenser is cleverly telling his reader that his work will be deliberately foggy to some readers, but to the "initiated," Spenser is revealing some hidden message to which he has access as a poet magus with the ability to peer behind the veil of knowledge. In the fourth stanza of Book II's proem, Spenser further mocks those who would "more inquyre" of "faery lond" and would "admyre" what his senses would reveal; rather, he should follow the lead of Spenser, the poet, who is the "hound" leading the reader through the tangled thicket of the poem "By certein signes here sett in sondrie place" (II.Proem.4). Spenser is thus the Ariadne who will lead his reader through the world of signs in which the reader could easily become lost or confused or miss the hidden meaning. He further tells Elizabeth to "pardon" him, for he will "enfold / In couert vele and wrap in shadowes light" the "glory" of Elizabeth that his poem contains and that would otherwise dazzle Elizabeth with "exceeding light" (II. Proem.5). It is not, however, merely Elizabeth's own glorious ancestry that Spenser will reveal: the poet also sees his poem as a window into another world, a world that Spenser says in the proem to Book VI is full of "perfect things" (VI.Proem.5). It is not that Spenser is a philosopher teaching a pupil knowledge via dialectics; rather, he is a Promethean, poet-magus, unveiling hidden truths to a reader being initiated into the mysteries.

Conclusion

Spenser scholar and biographer Andrew Hadfield is said to have humorously remarked that Edmund Spenser's *Faerie Queene* is "the only book no one has ever read." Hadfield's alleged remark speaks, not simply to the archaic language that Spenser employs in the poem, but to the sheer immensity of what is one of the longest verse works in the English language. At the same time, Hadfield's tongue-in-cheek comment points to the complexity of Spenser's thought. In his "endlesse worke," Spenser employs a host of different concepts and figures drawn from a number of often conflicting theological and philosophical schools. Within this tangled thicket of thought, Spenser appears to employ a form of Socratic irony revived by Renaissance Platonists who found themselves drawn to the ritual or magical elements of the Platonic tradition. In their works, these thinkers argued that the enlightened man or woman had the ability to peer behind the veil of truth and then communicate that truth to specific adepts and disciples. While Spenser utilizes this image of the poet magus with the privileged ability to unveil truth with varying degrees of confidence in the poem, in the "Two Cantos of Mutabilitie," Spenser appears to abandon his previous confidence and embraces some form of Christian fideism in which access to divine truths is obtainable via humble supplication and not the pride of a poet magus.

Georgia Southwestern State University

Edwardian Evangelicalism in Queen Elizabeth's Reign: William Baldwin's *Funeralles of King Edward The Sixt*

Scott Lucas

SOMETIME in 1560, in the second or early in the third year of Queen Elizabeth's reign, a work appeared in booksellers' stalls that sought to return readers to events of seven years past. This was William Baldwin's *Funeralles of King Edward the Sixt*, a small volume composed of three poems, each inspired by the loss in July 1553 of the sixteen-year-old evangelical English monarch Edward VI.[1] The first piece in the collection was a poetic narrative of the causes and progression of Edward VI's life-ending illnesses, which Baldwin presented in a cosmic setting comprising God, Christ, and two allegorical agents of divine will. The second poem presented a warning to England that its sins have stirred God's anger, and the third offered an admiring epitaph of the late king.

Baldwin was a strong evangelical, and the publication of a work such as the *Funeralles*, which seemed focused squarely on what for

---

1 William Baldwin, *The Funeralles of King Edward the sixt: Wherin are declared the causers and causes of his death* (London: Thomas Marshe, 1560). The work is no. 1243 in Alfred Pollard, G. R. Redgrave, William Jackson, F. S. Ferguson, and Katherine Pantzer, eds., *A Short-Title Catalogue of Books Printed in England, Scotland, & Ireland and of English Books Printed Abroad, 1475–1640*, 2nd ed., 3 vols. (London: Bibliographical Society, 1976–91) [hereafter *STC*]. It is likely that Baldwin's *Funeralles* appeared earlier rather than later in the year 1560, since its printer Thomas Marshe received a license to produce the work on January 24, 1560. See Edward Arber, ed., *A Transcript of the Registers of the Company of Stationers of London: 1554–1640 AD*, 5 vols. (London, 1875–77), 1:126.

Elizabethan Protestants was the highly traumatic loss of Edward, and the godly reform carried out in his name between 1547 and 1553 may have appeared an odd publication choice to book buyers at the opening of a new reign. After all, England had just emerged from five years of rule by Queen Mary I. Her guidance of England back to the papal fold in January 1555 had been widely repugnant to advanced evangelicals; her government's execution of over 280 Protestants in the last three years of her rule, of course, was even more so. In 1560, over a year into a new Protestant reign, one might expect an evangelical such as Baldwin to publish a hopeful, forward-looking work and not one asking readers to revisit the trauma of King Edward's loss.

Even more baffling was Baldwin's aim in creating the narrative section of his work. The book is titled *The Funeralles of King Edward the Sixt. Wherein are declared the causers and causes of his death* (sig. A1r). The title's suggestion that it would reveal to readers an accurate account of the king's demise was reinforced by Baldwin's preface to the collection, which declares "Great hath been the doubt among many, ever since the death of our late vertuous soverayne Lorde King Edward the syxt, by what meane he dyed and what were the causes of his death. This doubte is fully resolved in this booke, penned before his corse was buryed, & endeauoured since by many meanes to have had been printed: but such was the time, that it could not be brought to passe" (sig. A1v).

Certainly, there had been controversy about how King Edward came to his end, with at least some believing that he had been poisoned by the chief nobleman of the time, John Dudley, Duke of Northumberland.[2] Nevertheless, Baldwin did not seek to present a sober and objective exploration of the subject. While he described in moving detail the symptoms and growth of Edward's illness, few seeking objective knowledge of Edward's death could believe Baldwin's fanciful claim that Edward's trouble began with a menacing supernatural creature named Crazy Cold, who lived in a cave in the polar region and who flew down to court on God's command to sicken King Edward by sliding down Edward's esophagus to cause mischief to the king's stomach and lungs, mischief brought

---

2 Chris Skidmore, *Edward VI: The Lost King of England* (London: Phoenix, 2007), 258–59.

to a tragic conclusion only when a personified Death traveled to Greenwich Palace reluctantly to stab Edward with his dart (sigs. B1r, B3r–v).

One might ask, then, what might have been the purpose of Baldwin's decision to release this seemingly backward-looking and tragic poetic collection at the opening of Queen Elizabeth's reign. This essay will argue that Baldwin, while looking to the past for his poetic subject, in fact had his eyes set as much upon Queen Elizabeth's unfolding rule in issuing this publication as he did on the end of King Edward and his reign. Baldwin's poem is less an accurate account of Edward's last days than it is a stirring endorsement of the religious and economic beliefs of the most zealous evangelicals of King Edward's period, men whose actions and doctrines had come under doubt even in the Edwardian period and certainly during the Marian period that followed it. In the first years of Queen Elizabeth's rule, vanguard evangelicals, particularly those who had returned from exile under Mary, agitated for Protestant religious practices more advanced than those endorsed by the Elizabethan Act of Uniformity of 1559.[3] Baldwin's 1560 publication, by contrast, offers a vigorous argument for preservation of the authorized religion established in Edward's last years in power, and it urges a revival of precisely the sort of Edwardian commonwealth movement that had become discredited first in the wake of the 1549 rebellions and then all but lost during Mary's reign. For Baldwin, Edward VI's reign was not a failed period that must be left to the past. Instead, he offers King Edward and the reforms championed in his time as models for Elizabethan governors, and he warns that God himself will wreak vengeance if England does not embrace the program of social and religious reform he promotes.

Baldwin employed his *Funeralles* to promote social and religious reform initially in the weeks after Edward's death, when he composed at least two of its poems, and once again in Elizabeth's reign, when he brought it before the public. To do so, he inserts copious

---

3 Patrick Collinson, *The Elizabethan Puritan Movement* (Berkeley: Univ. of California Press, 1967), 29–55; Norman Jones, *The Birth of the Elizabethan Age* (Oxford: Blackwell, 1993), 48–65; Andrew Pettegree, "The Marian Exiles and the Elizabethan Settlement," in *Marian Protestantism: Six Studies* (Aldershot: Scolar Press, 1996), 141–50.

amounts of religious, social, and economic criticism in a text purporting in its title to focus solely on the young king's sickness and death. The entire second poem in the collection is given over to an excoriating critique of the English people, but even in the first poem, which presents Baldwin's fanciful account of how Edward died, the author lards his text with evangelically inflected critiques of the behavior of Edward's subjects.

The first poem in the collection opens with an account of a purported discussion in heaven between God and Christ concerning the depraved moral state of England and the English people. Baldwin's God bitterly condemns the current state of England not for the reforms its godly King has sought to institute in his realm but for the wicked refusal of the English people to accept them. Full of woe and wrath, God expresses his desire for a wholesale punishment of Edward's subjects. The Lord had made England "his wurd and chosens resting place," Baldwin declares, and he had given it a king "of such a godly minde / As seldom erst he elswhere had assinede" (sigs. A1v–A2r). So far have the English fallen short in adopting the Lord's and Edward's example that God feels the only remedy for their wickedness is "to destroy them all, / The yong, the old, the myghty with the small" (sig. A2r).

In response to Christ's request that he consider mercy, God angrily rehearses a litany of English sins, focusing specifically on those practiced by the political "heads" of the kingdom, whom he accuses, along with wealthy landowners and merchants, of a host of crimes, including enriching themselves with the church property recently expropriated for the purpose of succoring the poor, taking clerical income through impropriation and putting it to their own use, charging exorbitant rents, buying up and enclosing land, hoarding grain, and exploiting orphans of wealthy families in order to enjoy their incomes (sigs. A2v–A3r). Not only do such greedy acts cause dearth and economic ruin, God laments, but they undermine his own divinely appointed religious reforms, making Englishmen and women who might otherwise embrace evangelical ideas stick to their old, unreformed religious traditions, since they see those evangelical governors who rule in King Edward's name as self-serving hypocrites (sig. A3r–v). In deference to his son's concern for those few virtuous souls in England, however, God decides not utterly to destroy the English people if they persist in their wickedness but instead to strip them of his most precious gift, their pious King Edward (sig. A4r). Baldwin presents God to his readers as an Old Testament figure of anger and punishment, one who will eagerly visit his just wrath not merely on individual sinners but on an entire nation, unless his "chosen" people, as Baldwin characterizes the sixteenth-century English, walk in his ways.

The execrations of economic injustice and abuse of the church by the rich and powerful that Baldwin puts in God's mouth offer much the same sort of criticism that was advanced by the loose group of Edwardian evangelical authors traditionally called the Commonwealth men. Edwardian authors and preachers such as Robert Crowley, John Hales, Hugh Latimer, and Thomas Lever argued forcefully against economic self-interest, promoting charity, equity (though not equality) among the social classes, and religious reformation, while denouncing self-interest, profit-taking, enclosing of arable land, and the sort of false dealing they saw infecting economic relations between rich and poor. Whereas Edward VI's Lord Protector Edward Seymour, first Duke of Somerset, was understood by many such writers to have been sympathetic to their economic and religious causes, these same authors and ministers execrated those powerful nobles who ruled in King Edward's name after Somerset's deposition in October 1549. While the newly ascendant John Dudley, first Earl of Warwick and, later, Duke of Northumberland, continued religious reforms in England, many charged him and others who ruled in King Edward's name of only paying lip service to evangelical ideals, using them primarily as a cover to enrich themselves.[4]

The Commonwealth writers and their movement came to be discredited in the eyes of many of the upper classes, who blamed

---

4 Representative expressions of Edwardian Commonwealth thought can be found in R. H. Tawney and Eileen Powers, eds., *Tudor Economic Documents: Volume III, Pamphlets, Memoranda, and Literary Extracts* (London: Longmans, 1924). See also Robert Crowley, *The Select Works of Robert Crowley*, ed. J. W. Cooper (London, 1872). For evangelical anger at Dudley and his adherents in the last years of Edward's reign, see W. K. Jordan, *Edward VI: The Threshold of Power* (London: George Allen & Unwin, 1970), 373–75, 386; Diarmaid MacCulloch, *Thomas Cranmer: A Life* (New Haven, CT: Yale Univ. Press, 1996), 531–33.

their provocative, often angry calls for reform as threats to the social order and even as causes of the terrifying 1549 popular risings that sought economic reform. Fears of ongoing upheaval and the strong evangelical tenor of the Edwardian Commonwealth writings made them all but disappear in Mary's reign. Baldwin uses his 1560 collection to offer a new endorsement to Elizabethan readers of the commonwealth movement. Far from seeing the abuses denounced in Edward's reign as problems of the past, Baldwin, in publishing the *Funeralles*, warns Elizabethan readers that the moral and economic sins of injustice and self-love persist even in Elizabeth's reign. God's anger at such transgressions remains, and thus the same providential punishment that resulted in godly King Edward being taken from his subjects will happen to Queen Elizabeth as well, if Elizabethan subjects do not adopt the Commonwealth principles of the Edwardian period he revives.

Baldwin drives this point home in the second poem of the *Funeralles*, titled "An Exhortacion to the repentaunce of sinnes, and amendment of life, which were the cause of the kinges death, & wil be the destruction of the Realme, if God be not the more mercifull vnto us." It is not clear when Baldwin wrote this poem, which admonishes that, without amendment, God will take from England Edward's sister the queen just as he did Edward the king (sigs. C1r-C2v). While his preface warns that it will be Queen Elizabeth's death that God will bring about if England does not reform its sinful practices, Baldwin also states in that same preface that the entire "book" before readers was "penned before [Edward's] corpse was buried," that is, before August 8, 1553, when the funeral rites—delayed by the initial proclamation of Lady Jane Grey as queen and the time needed to establish Mary I in power—finally took place.[5] The queen at that time, of course, was Mary I, in her first month of rule. While Mary's adherence to traditional church practices, most notably the Latin service and the Mass, throughout Edward's reign was well known, Baldwin may have hoped that, in the wake of her contested, tumultuous accession to the throne of an evangelical

---

5 For King Edward's funeral, see Jennifer Loach, *Edward VI* (New Haven, CT: Yale Univ. Press, 1999), 167–69.

kingdom, Mary might well have determined it most prudent not to disturb the religious practices established by her brother's church.[6]

No matter if he wrote the second poem under Queen Mary or under Mary's sister, Baldwin published it in Queen Elizabeth's reign, and his decision to do so was born of an urgent desire to admonish England against indulging in the same sins that, he claims, led God to take King Edward. The broad program of social reform urged by the Edwardian Commonwealth men must be taken up again, his "Exhortacion" insists. Now that the English church has been re-established, the debilitation of religious charity and the despoiling of the newly restored church by greedy secular men that took place in Edward's reign must not start up once more, for, Baldwin insists, "that was the cause of the kings death in deede / And will be his heirs to, without better heede" (sig. C1r). Magistrates must resist corruption and administer their offices for the benefit of the realm. Merchants must not devote themselves to personal enrichment and selling of vain wares that, according to Baldwin, "serve to no purpose save bredyng up sin." Instead, they must make a fresh start under Elizabeth and sell only necessary goods and foodstuffs at reasonable prices (sigs. C1v–C2r). Rapacious enclosures of arable

---

6 For one hopeful expectation in the wake of Edward's death that Mary would preserve reformed religion, see Richard Taverner's *An Oration gratulatory made vpon the ioyfull proclaiming of the moste noble princes Quene Mary Quene of Englande* (London: John Day, 1553; not in *STC*). In this short work, Taverner notes that many evangelicals would be less fearful of the prospect of Mary's accession "if they mighte be assured, that the true religion of Christe, whych is nowe receyued into thys realme, myghte, throughe hir graciouse goodness, be retyened & kept styll." In response to them, Taverner confidently declares "I nothing doubt, but that all lawes, concerninge religio[n], made uppon iust and godlye groundes by aucthority of Parlyamente, in ye time of hir graces father of noble memorye kynge Henrye the eiyght, or which were made sithe[n]s that time, or that here after shalbe made, by like authority, and vpon like good, iust and godly grou[n]des hir highnes wyl confyrme, ratify, and establishe" (sigs. A5v–A6r). In point of fact, Mary's government officially maintained the 1552 Act of Uniformity until December 1553, when parliament returned England to the traditionalist religious practices followed in Henry VIII's last days (1 Mary, stat. 2, c.2). Papal authority over the English church was restored by statute in January 1555 (1 & 2 Philip and Mary, c.8).

land must not resume, rents must remain reasonable, and the practice of exploiting orphans of wealthy parents for the money they can bring cannot take place in Elizabeth's reign. Instead of reinstituting the sinful practices of the past, each man and woman must use this new opportunity to "aske God forgevenes, and make recompens / To those he hath harmed through any offence" (sig. C2v). Appearing in the opening years of Elizabeth's reign, Baldwin's text argues for a complete new moral and economic start in England, now that God has bestowed on the realm once more a godly monarch to rule it. The alternative would be God's angry removal from England of a beloved and virtuous ruler, this time Queen Elizabeth.

Economic reform, Baldwin continues, must go hand in hand with religious reform. In the troubled period after Elizabeth's accession, when the queen had to work carefully not to alienate too much on the one hand her religiously traditionalist subjects and on the other the enthusiastic, returning evangelical exiles who clamored for ecclesiastical reform even beyond that undertaken in Edward's reign, Baldwin offers a strong argument in favor of maintaining in Elizabeth's reign the state of English religion at the end of Edward's rule, when the second Act of Uniformity and the 1552 prayer book abolished the mass, rejected the doctrine of the real presence, and stripped (Baldwin would say cleansed) the church even of many of the remaining traditional religious practices preserved in the 1549 prayer book. Baldwin's chief opposition is to those who continue to insist on the doctrine of the real presence of Christ in the consecrated host. This doctrine was indeed one of the most passionate points of controversy in Edward's reign and beyond and, in confronting it, the 1559 parliament sought to tread lightly when creating the new Elizabethan teaching on this subject. In constructing the Elizabethan Act of Uniformity, parliament adopted for the new reign most of the contents of the reformed 1552 prayer book, but it did not let that text's complete rejection of Christ's presence in the communion wafer stand. Instead, it walked a fine line, combining the language of the 1549 prayer book, which preserved the idea of the real presence, with that of the 1552 prayer book, which presented the Eucharist as a commemoration only of Christ's sacrifice. After much dispute, parliament declared the language to be used at the presentation of the wafer to communicants to be "The bodie of our Lord Jesu Christ, which was given for thee, preserve thy body and soule into everlastinge life, and take and eate this, in remembraunce that Christ died for thee, and feede on him in thine heart by faith, with thanksgevynge."[7]

The ambiguous language, combining the 1549 prayer book's declaration of the real presence with the 1552 prayer book's declaration that the Eucharist was an act of remembrance, may have ultimately satisfied the majority of worshippers, but it would not satisfy William Baldwin. Baldwin uses the *Funeralles* to urge readers to reject completely the doctrine of transubstantiation and the idea of the sacrifice of the mass. Those Catholic and traditionalist priests who assert the real presence of Christ's body in the wafer commit "fowl dirogacion / of Christ his manhode, his merites and passion" (sig. C1v). Christ's body is in heaven, the Bible tells us. To claim that Christ's body is at once in heaven and, somehow, in every communion wafer is a contradiction of natural law—such a mystical claim does not recognize the humanity of Christ, his taking on of a natural body in all of its physical limitations to sacrifice himself for humans' sins. Moreover, the claim that Christ's body undergoes a new sacrifice at every mass denigrates the idea that his original sacrifice on the cross was sufficient to achieve our salvation. To drive his point home, Baldwin even has God himself denounce to Christ during their dialogue "such as would thy manhode spoyle / And rob from thee the merite of your toyle [Christ's passion]" (sig. A3r). Baldwin lumps the mass and the doctrine of the Real Presence together with other traditionalist beliefs as "popishe errours," and he warns that their continued tolerance in the realm by conservative English ministers and worshippers alike in Edward's reign, even when such beliefs were supposedly abolished by statute, "was the cause of the kings death in dede / And will be his heires to, without better hede" (sig. C1v).

Baldwin ends his "Exhortacion" with a declaration of the blanket culpability for the loss of the young king of all who lived through Edward's reign; his publication of this poem in 1560 stands as a plea to England's people to adopt the Commonwealth and advanced

---

7 J. E. Neale, *Elizabeth I and her Parliaments, 1559–1581* (London: Jonathan Cape, 1953), 78; Brian Cummings, ed., *the Book of Common Prayer: The Texts of 1549, 1559, and 1662* (Oxford: Oxford Univ. Press, 2011), 137.

Edwardian evangelical doctrines of Edward's reign, in order not to experience the loss of such a godly monarch once again. "Sith we are all already... gilty of murder," Baldwin asks readers to accept:

> Ceas we all for Gods sake, to sin any furder,
> O sleye not our Soverayne, our most noble Queen,
> Whose match in vertue hath seldom be seen,
> But pray the almighty her life to defend.
> Repent, recompence, pray, pay, and amend,
> For if our sins send her to her brother,
> Swift vengeance will folow, let none look for other. (sig. C2v)

The 1559 Act of Uniformity established the 1552 prayer book, with some modifications, as the official liturgy of the church, but a large number in England remained unhappy with the return of the realm to the most evangelically advanced doctrine of Edward's reign. Elizabeth herself was said to have preferred the Augsburg confession of the Lutherans to the tenets in force at Edward's death, and, as Christopher Haigh and others have noted, many in England continued to preserve the abolished traditional rites, ceremonies, and practices long after the Elizabethan settlement of religion was made.[8] Baldwin's decision in 1560 to resurrect his 1553 work on Edward's death seeks to reinforce the return to Edwardian evangelicalism in religion, with the added call for the re-adoption of the Commonwealth movement.

Publishing this work was just part of Baldwin's renewed commitment to the reformation of religion under Queen Elizabeth. In the very year his *Funeralles* appeared, Baldwin abandoned his lifelong profession as a printer to take holy orders (January 1560). His installation as rector of London's St. Michael le Querne church, which stood directly across from St. Paul's cathedral, in June 1561, allowed him a prominence among London clerics, and such was his skill as an orator that Bishop Grindal invited Baldwin to deliver a

---

[8] Jones, *Birth of the Elizabethan Age*, 17–35; Hirofumi Horie, "The Lutheran Influence on the Elizabethan Settlement, 1558–1563," *Historical Journal* 34, no. 3 (1991): 520–25; Christopher Haigh, *English Reformations: Religion, Politics, and Society under the Tudors* (Oxford: Oxford Univ. Press, 1993); Eamon Duffy, *The Stripping of the Altars: Traditional Religion in England, 1400–1580* (New Haven, CT: Yale Univ. Press, 1992).

sermon at Paul's Cross in September 1563. Baldwin used the opportunity to denounce Roman Catholicism, it seems, and to call for all unrepentant Marian bishops still held under arrest to be quickly executed. How much Baldwin might have altered his Edwardian beliefs manifested in the *Funeralles* in the ensuing controversies of the English church and in the rise of the Puritan movement unfortunately will never be known. He died of the plague just days after delivering his Paul's Cross sermon.[9] His publication of two more works in the wake of the *Funeralles*, namely *Beware the Cat* (1561) and the second edition of *A Mirror for Magistrates* (1563), shows that he continued to devote himself to attacks on religious traditionalism, particularly the Mass, and to commonwealth reform. Released in 1560, the *Funeralles* would be but one salvo in his battle for the hearts, minds, and souls of the Elizabethan people.

The Citadel

---

9 On Baldwin's last years, see Scott Lucas, "The Birth and Later Career of the Author William Baldwin (d. 1563)," *Huntington Library Quarterly* 79, no. 1 (2016): 149–62.

The Religious Dynamics of Robert Herrick's "Rex Tragicus"

Paul J. Stapleton

PERHAPS because of Robert Herrick's place among the Cavalier poets—he once wrote of Charles I, "War, which before was horrid, now appears / Lovely in you, brave Prince of Cavaliers!"—an explicitly religious poem like Herrick's "Good Friday: Rex Tragicus, or Christ Going to His Crosse" has been largely situated by critics in a seventeenth-century political context.[1] In arguably the most in-depth treatment of the poem to date, "Robert Herrick's 'Rex Tragicus' and the 'Troublesome Times,'" Thomas Moisan interprets the poem as a meditation on Charles I, regarding the focus on a *rex tragicus* as a foreboding of the Stuart king's looming execution at the hands of the Cromwellians in 1649.[2] This is not to say Moisan ignores religious dynamics in the poem, given that he also addresses its relation to the medieval Passion Play tradition as well as to the religiopolitical jeremiad of William Prynne's *Histriomastix* (1632), but Moisan's primary thrust is the political. In this essay, however, I will remain focused on the religious, specifically on what John N. Wall has called "English religious identity," which will be discussed in terms of (1) English spiritual practices,

---

1 Excerpt from "To the King, Upon his comming with his Army into the West." All Herrick poetry is taken from Tom Cain and Ruth Connolly, eds., *The Complete Poetry of Robert Herrick*, vol. 1 (Oxford: Oxford Univ. Press, 2013). On political readings, see Thomas Moisan, "Robert Herrick's 'Rex Tragicus' and the 'Troublesome Times,'" *Viator* 21 (1990): 349–84, and Marlin Blaine, "A Note on the Title of Herrick's *Rex Tragicus*," *English Language Notes* 38 (2000): 30–33.
2 Moisan, "Robert Herrick's 'Rex Tragicus,'" 377–84.

(2) topical matters related to English church history, and (3) the *Book of Common Prayer*.[3] In terms of English spiritual practices, it has been suggested that "Rex Tragicus" exemplifies the meditative poetic method first articulated by Louis Martz in his well-known 1954 work *The Poetry of Meditation*.[4] Martz argues that seventeenth-century English poets were greatly influenced by Continental spirituality, especially as articulated by Ignatius Loyola in his *Spiritual Exercises* (1548), where believers are directed to explore the four gospels using the fullness of their imaginations, entering into the narratives via formal meditations, or "exercises," mentally conjuring the events of the gospels in relation to the senses so as to experience the life of Christ on a deeply personal level.[5]

In line with Martz's thesis, "Rex Tragicus" draws upon miscellaneous features from the gospels drawn from Matthew 27, Mark 15, Luke 23, and John 19. Thus, in the poem, we find Herrick meditating upon the Passion of Christ, but also incorporating textual details from the Passion narratives, mostly taken from John 19, the gospel for Good Friday in the Book of Common Prayer:[6]

> Put off Thy Robe of Purple, then go on
> To the sad place of execution:
> Thine houre is come; and the Tormentor stands
> Ready, to pierce Thy tender Feet, and Hands.
> Long before this, the base, the dull, the rude,   5
> Th'inconstant, and unpurged Multitude
> Yawne for Thy coming; some e're this time crie,
> How He deferres, how loath He is to die!

---

3 For a discussion of the concept, see John N. Wall, "Crashaw, Catholicism, and Englishness: Defining Religious Identity," in *Renaissance Papers 2004*, ed. C. Cobb and M. T. Hester (Rochester, NY: Camden House, 2004), 107–26.

4 Roger Rollin, *Robert Herrick* (New York: Twayne Publishers, 1966), 157. In explaining Ignatian meditation, Rollin focuses on Herrick's "His Meditation upon Death," not "Rex Tragicus."

5 See Louis Martz, *The Poetry of Meditation* (New Haven, CT: Yale Univ. Press, 1954), 25–30.

6 All references to the Book of Common Prayer are taken from the 1559 edition found at *Online Anglican Resources*, http://justus.anglican.org/resources/bcp/1559/BCP_1559.htm.

> Amongst this scumme, the Souldier, with his speare,
> And that sowre Fellow, with his vineger,   10
> His spunge, and stick, do ask why Thou dost stay? (*ll.* 1–11)

Here, we find Passion fixtures like the "robe of purple" given to Christ by the soldiers (*l.* 1); the "multitude" gathered at Calvary (*l.* 6); "the Souldier, with his speare" (*l.* 9); and the sponge soaked with vinegar (*ll.* 10–11). Later in the poem, we find the placard on the cross designating Jesus as "king" of the Jews (*l.* 28); the "theeves" crucified on either side of Christ (*l.* 23); and of course, "the crosse" itself (*l.* 17) [See Addendum].

We also discover the narrator inserting himself into the scene, personally speaking to Christ and self-identifying with other figures who are present at the crucifixion. Such an imaginative engagement with the Passion narrative reflects Ignatius's recommendation in *The Spiritual Exercises*, where he advises believers to "imagine Christ our Lord suspended on the cross before you, and converse with him in a colloquy."[7] Thus, in "Rex Tragicus," Herrick uses the second person *thee* as his narrator addresses Christ directly as well as the first person *we* to indicate those, like the narrator himself, who are presented collectively to Christ as "Thy Lovers":

> And we (Thy Lovers) while we see Thee keep
> The Lawes of Action, will both sigh, and weep;
> And bring our Spices, to embalm Thee dead;
> That done, wee'l see Thee sweetly buried. (*ll.* 36–39)

Here, the allusion is to the gospel of John and its description of those who buried Christ, that is, Joseph of Arimathea and the pharisee Nicodemus.[8] Herrick, no doubt, would have seen himself in both these figures, not only as a matter of piety, as some critics have

---

7 Martz, *The Poetry of Meditation*, 55. For the text, see *The Spiritual Exercises of Saint Ignatius*, trans. G. Ganss, SJ (Chicago: Loyola Univ. Press, 1992), 42.

8 John 19: 38–40: "And after this Joseph of Arimathaea, being a disciple of Jesus, but secretly for fear of the Jews, besought Pilate that he might take away the body of Jesus: and Pilate gave him leave. He came therefore, and took the body of Jesus. And there came also Nicodemus, which at the first came to Jesus by night, and brought a mixture of myrrh and aloes, about an hundred pound weight. Then took they the body of

suggested, but also in terms of his English religious identity, given that Joseph of Arimathea and Nicodemus had each come to represent topical components of that identity in seventeenth-century England.[9] According to the dominant strain of early modern English church historiography, Joseph of Arimathea was the original apostle to Britain.[10] We find such an account, for example, in John Foxe's *Book of Martyrs*:

> I take of the testimony of Gildas, our countreyman, who in his history affirmeth plainely, that Britayne receaued the Gospell in the tyme of Tiberius the Emperour, vnder whom Christ suffered. Lib. De victoria, Aurelii Ambrosii. And sayth moreouer, Ioseph of Arimathie after the dispersion of the Iewes, was sent of Philip the Apostle from Fraunce to Britayne, about the yeare of our Lord. 63. and here remayned in this land all hys tyme: and so with his fellowes, layd the first foundation of Christian fayth among the Britayne people.[11]

For Herrick, the term "we (Thy lovers)" would refer, therefore, to the faithful descendants of the first apostle to Britain, people like himself, descendants of Joseph of Arimathea, the gospel figure who was

---

Jesus, and wound it in linen clothes with the spices, as the manner of the Jews is to bury" (KJV).

9 Robert Deming remarks on the "simple piety" of verses 36–39 in *Ceremony and Art: Robert Herrick's Poetry* (The Hague: Mouton & Co. N.V., Publishers, 1974), 76; and Don Cameron Allen on the "childish religiosity" of Herrick's Noble Numbers in *Image and Meaning* (Baltimore: Johns Hopkins Press, 1968), 138.

10 See John Bale, *The Actes of Englysh Votaryes* (Wesel: [Mierdman], 1546), 13ᵛ–14ʳ, Early English Books Online (EEBO); and Polydore Vergil, *Anglica Historia* (1555), ed. and trans. Dana F. Sutton (Birmingham: Univ. of Birmingham, 2010), 2.7. Bale cites Polydore Vergil and Gildas as his sources.

11 John Foxe, *The Acts and Monuments Online* (*TAMO*), ed. David Loades (Sheffield: Univ. of Sheffield Press, 2011), 2.130 (1576 edition). Foxe draws on John Bale.

considered by members of the English church as the true founder of the original church in England.[12]

As for Nicodemus, among sixteenth- and seventeenth-century English religious polemicists, the derogatory terms "Nicodemus" and "Nicodemite" referred to those who hid their true religious beliefs in the name of escaping persecution.[13] During the Civil Wars, Herrick, ordained a priest in 1623 and appointed a vicariate in 1629, was a victim of the Cromwellian purge of Laudians and royalists despite the fact that he had taken the official "Protestation" oath on behalf of his parish in the year 1642.[14] The oath stated that the parish was in accord with "the true reformed Protestant Religion" and "the power and privilege of Parliaments."[15] Arguably, Herrick would have considered himself a Nicodemite for having sworn the oath in the first place, a pledge the Cromwellians clearly regarded as spurious because Herrick was ousted from his clerical office in 1646.

Finally, I would like to consider "Rex Tragicus" in relation to Good Friday scriptural readings prescribed in the Book of Common Prayer (1559), which Herrick engages, albeit indirectly, through a process akin to medieval typology. The basis for my claim is Herrick's Christus-Roscius analogy, where the poet-narrator says to Christ, "Thou art that Roscius" (*l.* 19). Such an analogy would seem a dangerous tack for Herrick, given that in some circles in early modern England, Roscius was considered anything but Christ-like as we find him variously identified as "Roscius the Stager, (that honest Nicodemus)" and even as "the Master Hypocrite of all."[16] For an

---

12 This tradition was not without religious controversy as English Catholics viewed Saint Augustine as the first apostle to the English, a tradition promulgated by Bede and in the late sixteenth century, Thomas Stapleton. See Paul Stapleton, "Pope Gregory and the *Gens Anglorum,*" *Renaissance Papers 2008*, ed. C. Cobb (Rochester, NY: Camden House, 2009), 32–33.

13 See Alexandra Walsham, *Catholic Reformation in Protestant Britain* (Burlington, VT: Ashgate, 2014), especially the chapters "England's Nicodemites," 85–101, and "Ordeals of Conscience," 103–25.

14 Cain and Connolly, eds., *The Complete Poetry*, xxxviii, xli, liii-lv.

15 Ibid., liii.

16 Thomas Dekker, *Satiromastix* (London: Edward White, 1602), *ll.* 631–36, Project Gutenberg, https://www.gutenberg.org/files/49636/

educated English audience, however, I believe the Christus-Roscius analogy is tantamount to an invitation to interpret the Good Friday readings typologically in the light of the Roman actor Roscius, but referencing Ciceronian texts instead of the Old Testament. In his benchmark work on biblical typology, *From Shadows to Reality*, Jean Daniélou says "the essence of typology" is "to show how past [biblical] events are a figure of events to come."[17] Typological figures can best be understood via two concepts, *recirculatio* and *recapitulatio*.[18] As Peter Chrysologus explains *recirculatio*, the very same pathways (*cursus*) that lead to salvation are necessarily those that first led to death.[19] For example, he says, "Christ was crucified so that life might return through a tree because, through a tree, death had first come."[20] Typology, therefore, calls for resemblances that are contingent upon both similarities and differences. For Irenaeus, according to the concept of *recapitulatio*, Christ is the new Adam, re-enacting Adam's fall, but in an antithetical way to Adam.[21] As Irenaeus says, "Through his obedience on a tree," Christ effects "the recapitulation of the disobedience which occurred also

---

49636-h/49636-h.htm; and Lancelot Andrewes, XCVI. Sermons (London: George Miller, [1629]), 232, EEBO.

17 Jean Daniélou, *From Shadows to Reality: Studies in the Biblical Typology of the Fathers (Sacramentum Futuri)*, trans. Wulstan Hibberd (London: Burns & Oates, 1960), 12.

18 For a discussion of *recapitulatio*, see Daniélou, *From Shadows to Reality*, 30–47; for *recirculatio*, see G. M. Lukken, *Original Sin in the Roman Liturgy* (Leiden: Brill, 1973), 369–75.

19 Chrysologus's *Sermo* 142, On the Feast of the Annunciation, *Patrologia Latina Database*, ed. Jacques-Paul Migne (Alexandria, VA: Chadwyck-Healey, 1996), 52 col. 579B: "Audistis agi, ut homo cursibus eisdem quibus dilapsus fuerat ad mortem, rediret ad vitam." (You have heard it accomplished that man returns to life by the very same pathways by which he had fallen to death.). Translation is mine.

20 Chrysologus, *Sermo* 59, On the Creed, *PL*, ed. Migne, 52 col. 364A: "Crucifixus est. Ut quia per lignum mors venerat, rediret vita per lignum."

21 Daniélou, *From Shadows to Reality*, 30; and Lukken, *Original Sin*, 360–61.

via a tree."[22] Adam, the prefiguration of Christ, is recapitulated, or renewed, in Christ because Adam's disobedience is reversed.[23] In "Rex Tragicus," instead of the new Adam, Christ is figured as the "new" Roscius. The Christian deity is analogized as the Roman actor by means of a completely original typological relationship, seemingly peculiar to Herrick, which rests upon the positing of a new pathway, a new *cursus*, wherein the cross is no longer figured as a tree:

> The Crosse shall be Thy Stage; and Thou shalt there
> The spacious field have for Thy Theater.
> Thou art that Roscius, and that markt-out man,
> That must this day act the Tragedian. (*ll.* 17–20)

Here, the "crosse" from the Good Friday gospel reading becomes Christ's stage, which in the manner of the concept of *recirculatio*, allows Christ to become a player in the "theater," a "tragedian" just like Roscius. Christ's performance, however, goes beyond any earthly performance. As the narrator says to Christ, "Proceed, to act Thy Passion / To such an height, to such a period rais'd,/ As Hell, and Earth, and Heav'n may stand amaz'd" (*ll.* 29–31). In this way, Christ becomes the new tragedian, whose theater has cosmic proportions, a divine actor ("once a King / And God"—*ll.* 24–25), who can amaze "Hell, and Earth, and Heav'n." As we learn from the Good Friday reading from the epistle to the Hebrews, Christ, because of his action on the cross, "is set doune for ever on the righte hand of God; and from hencefoorth tarieth tyll his foes be made his footestoole. For with one offeryng hathe he made perfect for ever, them that are sanctified."[24] Christ's performance, therefore, far surpasses the "period" and "height" of any mortal actor like Roscius.

---

22 Irenaeus, *Libros Quinque adversus Haereses*, ed. W. Wigan Harvey, vol. 2 (Cambridge: Typis Academicis, 1857), 375 (Book 5.19.1): "Dominum [...] recapitulationem ejus quae in ligno fuit inobedientiae, per eam quae in ligno est obedientiam, facientem." Translation is mine.

23 Louis van Tongeren, *Exaltation of the Cross: Towards the Origins of the Feast of the Cross and the Meaning of the Cross in Early Medieval Liturgy* (Leuven: Peeters, 2000), 86–88.

24 Hebrews 10: 12–14, cited from the Book of Common Prayer (1559).

This is not to say that the reputation of Roscius was, in many cases, anything less than extraordinary. Roscius was a well-known figure in seventeenth-century England, primarily through the works of Cicero but also through countless early modern tracts.[25] Historically, Roscius was a first-century, BCE, contemporary of Cicero, mentioned in several of Cicero's works such as the *Pro Archia Poeta* and *De Natura Deorum*, texts which were promoted in early modern English humanist education.[26] In the *Pro Archia*, Cicero claims that Roscius was so renowned that "when he died an old man, nevertheless, on account of his surpassing artistry and sex appeal, it seemed altogether that he ought not to have died [qui cum esset senex mortuus, tamen propter excellentem artem ac venustatem videbatur omnino mori non debuisse]."[27] As an actor, he was apparently all but immortal. In *De Natura Deorum*, however, Roscius outshines the immortals as Cicero relates an anecdote about a poet who once wrote that Roscius seemed to him "more beautiful than a god [*deo pulchrior*]."[28] Critics have noted that such superlative attributes seem rather curious when equating Roscius with the sorrowful Christian deity dying on the cross.[29] Perhaps there is room for the analogy, however, if the Roscius of the *De Natura Deorum* is considered within the framework of Irenaeus's concept of *recapitulatio*.

Cicero's *De Natura Deorum* is essentially a theological treatise in the form of a dialogue that puts forth various Greco-Roman schools of thought on the relationship between the gods and humans, with an emphasis on the theologies of Epicureanism and Stoicism.[30] In the segment where Roscius is mentioned, the topic of conversation

---

25 See Allen, *Image and Meaning*, 147–49; and Moisan, "Robert Herrick's 'Rex Tragicus,'" 370–71. For an overview of Roscius in Latin literature, see "A Roman Actor—Quintus Roscius," *Eclectic Magazine* n.s. 7 (1868): 672–80.

26 See, for example, Roger Ascham, *The Scholemaster* (London: John Day, [1570]), 37v, EEBO.

27 Marcus Tullius Cicero, *Pro Archia Poeta*, ed. G. H. Nall (New York: St Martin's, 1901), 11 (sec. 17). Translation is mine.

28 Cicero, *De Rerum Natura: Book I*, ed. A. R. Dyck (Cambridge: Cambridge Univ. Press, 2003), 42 (sec. 79).

29 Allen, *Image and Meaning*, 149, uses the term "insolent."

30 Dyck, ed., *De Rerum Natura*, 5.

is the plausibility of deities having physical forms and bodies.[31] One of the interlocutors, a Skeptic named Cotta, doubts that any true deity would ever take on physical form (*forma*), including human form because, he says, even the most beautiful humans possess *maculas corporis*, that is, "stains of the body," or *vitia* ("flaws"). It is at this point that we are given the anecdote about Roscius being "more beautiful than a god."

Cotta, however, outright dismisses the anecdote because, he informs us, Roscius was also known to have *perversissimos oculos*, that is, his eyes were "very turned" or "squint eyed."[32] This physical trait of Roscius was well-known in early modern England, and in *The Arte of English Poesie* (1589), George Puttenham mentions it as the etiology for stage masks: "Because he was squint eyed and had a very vnpleasant countenance, and lookes which made him ridiculous or rather odious to the presence, he deuised these vizards to hide his owne ill fauored face."[33] In *De Natura Deorum*, Cotta uses the circumstance of Roscius's purported unpleasant countenance to gainsay the likelihood that any gods would ever become incarnate in flawed human bodies. For Cotta, such anthropomorphic beliefs are *absurda*.[34]

Of course, in the Christian tradition, human frailty is the very condition in which the deity is said to become incarnate. In the evening-prayer lesson for Good Friday, Isaiah 53, we learn of a Christ who is far from physically attractive or flawless.[35] As the text reads, "He hath no form nor comeliness; and when we shall see him, there is no beauty that we should desire him. He is despised and rejected of men; a man of sorrows."[36] Here the *recapitulatio* of Roscius is made complete in the Christ who lacks "form," "comeliness," and

---

31 Cicero, *De Rerum Natura*, 41 (sec. 74–77).
32 Ibid., 162.
33 George Puttenham, *The Arte of English Poesie* (London: Richard Field, 1589), 26, EEBO. For a discussion of the tradition, see Catharine Saunders, "The Introduction of Masks on the Roman Stage," *American Journal of Philology* (1911): 58–73.
34 Cicero, *De Rerum Natura*, 42 (sec. 81).
35 See "Proper Lessons to Be Read for the First Lessons Both at Morning Prayer and Evening Prayer: Holy Days."
36 Isaiah 53: 2–3 (KJV).

"beauty." It is as a despised and rejected "man of sorrows" that the deity becomes incarnate. Nevertheless, as the narrator of "Rex Tragicus" says to the dying Christ, "This Scene from Thee takes life and sense,/ And soule and spirit, plot, and excellence" (*ll*. 26–27). Christ is the new tragedian, the new Roscius.

In the end, Robert Herrick steeps his poem in English religious identity but in a way that does not shy away from syncretism. According to one adage about Roscius, "Euerye man (as saith the prouerbe) is Roscius in his owne facultie."[37] Apparently, Herrick was willing to recast the Christian deity as exemplifying "his owne facultie" well enough to be comparable to the man Roscius, a daring syncretism in much the same spirit of other early modern English poets—dare I say—like John Milton.[38]

Addendum

"Good Friday: Rex Tragicus, or, Christ Going to His Cross"

Put off Thy Robe of Purple, then go on
To the sad place of execution:
Thine houre is come; and the Tormentor stands
Ready, to pierce Thy tender Feet, and Hands.
Long before this, the base, the dull, the rude,   5
Th'inconstant, and unpurged Multitude
Yawne for Thy coming; some e're this time crie,
How He deferres, how loath He is to die!
Amongst this scumme, the Souldier, with his speare,
And that sowre Fellow, with his vineger,   10
His spunge, and stick, do ask why Thou dost stay?
So do the Skurfe and Bran too: Go Thy way,
Thy way, Thou guiltlesse man, and satisfie
By Thine approach, each their beholding eye.
Not as a thief, shalt Thou ascend the mount,   15

---

37 The proverb is quoted in Wawrzyniec Goslicki [Laurentius Grimalus], *The Counsellor Exactly Pourtraited* (London: Richard Bradocke, [1598]), 20, EEBO.

38 On Milton's syncretism, see for example, Anna Nardo, "Renaissance Syncretism and Milton's Convivial Sonnets," *Explorations in Renaissance Culture* 4 (1978): 32–42.

But like a Person of some high account:
The Crosse shall be Thy Stage; and Thou shalt there
The spacious field have for Thy Theater.
Thou art that Roscius, and that markt-out man,
That must this day act the Tragedian,   20
To wonder and affrightment: Thou art He,
Whom all the flux of Nations comes to see;
Not those poor Theeves that act their parts with Thee:
Those act without regard, when once a King,
And God, as Thou art, comes to suffering.   25
No, No, this Scene from Thee takes life and sense,
And soule and spirit, plot, and excellence.
Why then begin, great King! ascend Thy Throne,
And thence proceed, to act Thy Passion
To such an height, to such a period rais'd,   30
As Hell, and Earth, and Heav'n may stand amaz'd.
God, and good Angells guide Thee; and so blesse
Thee in Thy severall parts of bitternesse;
That those, who see Thee nail'd unto the Tree,
May (though they scorn Thee) praise and pitie Thee.   35
And we (Thy Lovers) while we see Thee keep
The Lawes of Action, will both sigh, and weep;
And bring our Spices, to embalm Thee dead;
That done, wee'l see Thee sweetly buried.

North Carolina Central University

Rewriting the Psalmist: Form and Gender in *A Meditation of a Penitent Sinner*

Mary Ruth Robinson

I N *A Meditation of a Penitent Sinner* (1560), Ann Lock urges her beloved to "dryve me not from thy face in my distresse," adding to her plea, "take not away the succour of thy sprite."[1] Yet, in a sonnet sequence devoted to the agony of longing, Lock speaks not to a human lover but to her God, and this impassioned plea to the object of her desire rewords merely a single verse of Psalm 51.[2] In *A Meditation of a Penitent Sinner*, Lock transforms the nineteen lines of Psalm 51 [See Appendix] into twenty-one sonnets. The *Meditation* is a striking sequence, one that challenges a number of critical commonplaces about authorship, gender, and the sonnet. While the *Meditation* has most frequently been studied alongside other examples of writing and metrical psalms by early modern women such as Mary Sidney Herbert's rhyme royal Psalm 51, the significance of Lock's choice of the sonnet—and the ways in which she makes use of the particular affordances of the sonnet sequence—remains relatively unexplored. This paper makes a case for closer attention

---

1 Anne Lock, *Sermons of John Calvin, vpon the songe that Ezechias made after he had bene sicke, and afflicted by the hand of God, conteyned in the 38. Chapter of Esay* (London, 1560), 13.4, 13.8. Quotations from Lock's sonnets are cited by sonnet number and line number; subsequent references to her poetry are cited parenthetically.

2 "Cast me not awaie from thy presence, and take not thine holie Spirit from me" (Ps. 51.11). All biblical quotations in this paper refer to the 1560 Geneva Bible unless otherwise specified. See the Appendix for the full text.

to the role of form in the *Meditation*. I begin by examining some of the context surrounding the sonnet sequence before looking at three poems that I suggest distinguish Lock not merely as poet but as sonneteer. Ultimately, I argue, Lock draws on two traditions yet deviates from both; she appropriates the voice of the psalmist and in doing so, complicates received narratives about the relationship of early modern women to the sonnet.

Of course, describing the *Meditation* as Lock's sonnet sequence is not uncontroversial, and while a full review of the decades-long debate surrounding authorship of this work is beyond the scope of this paper, it is impossible to discuss the sequence without first acknowledging that the authorship is indeed contested.[3] In 1560, *A Meditation of a Penitent Sinner* appeared in print appended to a volume of four translated sermons by John Calvin. Although the work's dedication to Katherine Brandon, the Duchess of Suffolk, bears only the mark "A.L." and no name appears on the title page, the translation of Calvin is almost certainly Lock's work.[4] The authorship of the sonnet sequence itself, however, is less clear. An unsigned introduction to the sequence claiming that "this meditation . . . was deliuered me by my frend with whom I knew I might be so bolde to vse & publishe it as pleased me" has generated considerable debate over the identity of this anonymous friend.[5] The Scottish minister John Knox corresponded with Lock for years, and Patrick Collinson identifies the sonnets as "Knox's work," while Jane E. A. Dawson finds the sonnets to "probably" be the work of Knox's friend Christopher Goodman.[6] Yet no strong evidence supports either theory, and in lieu of a more compelling alternative, scholars

---

3   My thanks to the attendees of the 80th Annual Meeting of the Southeastern Renaissance Conference, especially Robert E. Stillman and Eric Dunnum, for their lively and stimulating engagement with the authorship question.
4   For a thorough introduction to Lock and her oeuvre, see Susan M. Felch, ed., *The Collected Works of Anne Vaughan Lock* (Tempe, AZ: Renaissance English Text Society, 1999).
5   Lock, *Sermons of John Calvin*, 81.
6   Patrick Collinson, "Locke [*née* Vaughan; *other married names* Dering, Prowse], Anne," *Oxford Dictionary of National Biography*, September 23, 2004, accessed August 9, 2020, doi.org/10.1093/ref:odnb/69054. Jane E. A. Dawson, "Goodman, Christopher," *Oxford Dictionary of National*

have long treated Lock as the most likely author of the sequence.[7] The attribution of the poems to a friend may simply have been a fiction, a way for Lock to distance herself from the poems and avoid accusations of immodesty or as Deirdre Serjeantson convincingly argues, the charge of female preaching.[8]

In 2017, the authorship debate took on new life when Steven W. May identified Thomas Norton as the author of the *Meditation*. May's argument, while intriguing, seems to me, however, to move towards its conclusion with undue haste. As May himself notes, "No direct evidence links Norton and Anne Lock by 1560."[9] Moreover, while May claims that "Lock's denial of authorship should have sufficed to remove the *Meditation* from the list of her canonical works," his swift dismissal of the obstacles faced by early modern women writers is less than convincing.[10] Most importantly, Jake Arthur's recent critique of May's methodology strikes a serious blow against the Norton theory. May selected nine unusual words used by the author of the *Meditation* and, after searching the Early English

---

Biography, January 3, 2008, accessed August 8, 2020, doi.org/10.1093/ref:odnb/10975.

7 For the argument against Knox, see Roland Greene, "Anne Lock's *Meditation:* Invention Versus Dilation and the Founding of Puritan Poetics," in *Form and Reform in Renaissance England*, ed. Amy Boesky and Mary Thomas Crane (Newark: Univ. of Delaware Press, 2000), 153–70. For the argument against Goodman (and a strong argument in favor of Lock), see Deirdre Serjeantson, "Anne Lock's Anonymous Friend: 'A Meditation of a Penitent Sinner' and the Problem of Ascription," in *Enigma and Revelation in Renaissance English Literature*, ed. Helen Cooney and Mark S. Sweetnam (Dublin: Four Courts, 2012), 51–72.

8 See also Margaret P. Hannay, "'Unlock My Lipps': The *Miserere Mei Deus* of Anne Vaughan Lok and Mary Sidney Herbert, Countess of Pembroke," in *Privileging Gender in Early Modern England*, ed. Jean R. Brink (Kirksville, MO: Sixteenth Century Journal Publishers, 1993), 19–36; Patricia Pender, *Early Modern Women's Writing and the Rhetoric of Modesty* (New York: Palgrave Macmillan, 2012); and Rosalind Smith, *Sonnets and the English Woman Writer, 1560–1621: The Politics of Absence* (New York: Palgrave Macmillan, 2005).

9 Steven W. May, "Anne Lock and Thomas Norton's *Meditation of a Penitent Sinner*," *Modern Philology* 114, no. 4 (2017): 793–819, here 808.

10 Ibid., 794.

Books Online and Text Creation Partnership (EEBO-TCP), identified Norton as the only other writer to use all nine words. As Arthur demonstrates, however, May neglected spelling variants and thus vastly overestimated the rarity of these words.[11] As Arthur argues at length, not only do "methodological problems undercut May's evidence, but that evidence is already inadequate for the claim being made."[12]

I agree with Arthur's assessment: until new evidence emerges, Lock remains the most plausible author of the *Meditation*. More broadly, though, I am interested in the gender of the speaker of these poems, not just the gender of the author. If Norton (or Knox, or Goodman, or some other poet) wrote the *Meditation*, he did so by imagining a distinctly feminized speaker. Looking beyond authorship, therefore, this paper argues for renewed attention to the gendered voice of the sonnets and the ways in which their author explores the relationship between gender and form.

Early Modern Women and the Sonnet

A woman writer rewriting the psalms in the English Renaissance occupied a curious position: something more than translator, but perhaps something less than author. For both women and men in the sixteenth century, religious translation, including psalm translation, served as an acceptable literary activity, often in contrast to the writing or reading of secular poetry. This contrast was particularly pronounced in advice for young women. In the popular sixteenth-century conduct book *The Instruction of a Christian Woman*, for example, Juan Luis Vives writes that if a woman must learn to write, "Let not her example be voyde verses, nor wanton or trifling Songes, but some sadde sentence, prudent and chaste, taken out of the Scripture, or the sayinges of Philosophers."[13] In *The Chris-*

---

[11] Jake Arthur, "Anne Lock or Thomas Norton? A Response to the Reattribution of the First Sonnet Sequence in English," *Early Modern Women: An Interdisciplinary Journal* 16, no. 2 (2022): 213–36, esp. 219–25.

[12] Ibid., 225.

[13] Juan Luis Vives, *A verie fruitfull and pleasant booke, called the instruction of a christian woman . . . translated out of Latine into Englishe, by Richard*

tian mans closet, Barthélemy Batt offers similar guidance to fathers of daughters: "Let her first learne the Psalter or Psalmes of Dauid in méeter, which may withdrawe her minde from light and vaine songues, and baudie ballades."[14] The labor of translation, according to these and other conduct books, might serve to occupy a young woman's thoughts and free her from the infinite perils of her own mind. Translation was one possible literary activity for men, but in theory—though certainly not always in practice—it was set forth as the only possibility available to women. Psalm paraphrase, while a bolder act than literal translation, aligned with these norms.[15]

The sonnet, on the other hand, is a form associated with male desire, not the spiritual education of women. If the psalms epitomized the proper text for the woman reader, the sonnet far more closely resembled that dangerous alternative of wanton songs. Unlike their continental counterparts, English women very rarely wrote sonnets, most often appearing as subject rather than as author: artfully dismembered, worshipped or wept over, made muse and mistress. The work of Mary Wroth, the most prominent exception to this rule, only emphasizes the relative lack of English women's sonnets. Rosalind Smith, for example, describes women's sonnets before Wroth's *Pamphilia to Amphilanthus* as "anomalous exceptions";[16] Diana E. Henderson picks up the puzzle on the other side, asking, "But what happened to female sonneteering after Wroth?"[17]

Scholars have broadened this narrative of absence and exception by looking for sonnets in less expected places, as for example,

---

Hyrde (London, 1585), 28.

14 Barthélemy Batt, *The Christian mans closet Wherein is contained a large discourse of the godly training vp of children . . . nowe Englished by William Lowth* (London, 1581), 75.

15 For example, Edward Denny cited Mary Sidney Herbert's "heavenly lays" (or psalms) as evidence of her virtue in his attack on the "lascivious tales" of her niece, Mary Wroth—while, of course, not mentioning Sidney Herbert's secular translations. Josephine A. Roberts, *The Poems of Lady Mary Wroth* (Baton Rouge: Louisiana State Univ. Press, 1983), 34.

16 Smith, *Sonnets and the English Woman Writer*, 2.

17 Diana E. Henderson, "Where Had All the Flowers Gone? The Missing Space of Female Sonneteers in Seventeenth Century England," *Renaissance and Reformation* 35, no. 1 (2012): 139–65, here 140.

the sonnet that opens Elizabeth Cary's *Tragedy of Mariam*.[18] Much has been done, too, to complicate the narrative that Petrarchism is essentially about "a successful assertion of male power and the concomitant erasure of the female" and thus in some way inherently inaccessible to the early modern woman writer.[19] Yet the question of why more sixteenth- and seventeenth-century English women did not write sonnets remains. The *Meditation* sequence, if Lock's, written at such an early stage in the development of the English sonnet, can serve as a valuable tool for thinking through the uneasy relationship between gender and form.

Of course, the lived experiences of women writers were more complex than any list in a conduct book, and many women translated secular as well as religious texts with varying levels of freedom. The psalms were particularly well-suited for this free translation— or "paraphrase" (to use Lock's own term for the *Meditation*)—since "Christians had long been urged to treat the words of the psalmist as if they were their own."[20] Psalm translation enabled many women to explore authorship, including writers such as Anne Askew and Catherine Parr, placing them in the company of men undertaking similar translations like those by Myles Coverdale, Thomas Sternhold and John Hopkins, and Thomas Wyatt. Yet not one of those metrical psalms takes the shape of a sonnet.[21]

The lack of psalm-sonnets by 1560 is not entirely surprising, given the formal differences between psalms and sonnets. Philip Sidney captures one key distinction with his rather grudging note in *The Defence of Poesie* that the book of Psalms "is fully written

---

18 See Ilona Bell, "Private Lyrics in Elizabeth Cary's *Tragedy of Mariam*," in *The Literary Career and Legacy of Elizabeth Cary, 1613–1680*, ed. Heather Wolfe (New York: Palgrave Macmillan, 2007), 17–34.

19 Heather Dubrow, *Echoes of Desire: English Petrarchism and its Counterdiscourses* (Ithaca, NY: Cornell Univ. Press, 1995), 10.

20 Margaret P. Hannay, "'Wisdome the Wordes': Psalm Translation and Elizabethan Women's Spirituality," *Religion & Literature* 23, no. 3 (1991): 65–82, here 66.

21 In the Sidney Psalter, composed several decades after the *Meditation*, only two psalms appear as sonnets, Psalm 100 and Psalm 150, interestingly both by Mary Sidney Herbert rather than her brother.

in metre ... although the rules be not yet fully found."[22] Moreover, biblical Hebrew poetry rarely rhymes, and complex rhymes—like those that comprise a sonnet—occur especially infrequently. Instead, the "first and chief" characteristic of Hebrew poetry is parallelism, that is, the repetition of a single idea across lines.[23] Whereas a sonnet depends on movement like the sharp break of a *volta* or the sudden resolution of a final couplet, the psalms commonly consist of a single idea reiterated at length; they divide easily into categories such as communal lament, praise, or penitence.[24] Even more surprising than the dearth of psalm-sonnets, however, is the fact that the author of the *Meditation* chose to write twenty-one: the choice of form is as significant as it is unusual. The unexpected harmony found in the union of psalm translation and sonneteering, I believe, allowed the sonneteer to re-gender, and reimagine, the voice of the psalmist.

The Psalm-Sonnets of the *Meditation*

Crucially, if Anne Lock did author the *Meditation*, as I am claiming here, it is the first sonnet sequence ever written by an English woman, and indeed, the first English-language sonnet sequence whatsoever. Perhaps because of this significance, the rationale of the author of the *Meditation* in choosing the sonnet form has proven somewhat perplexing. The length of the sequence suggests purpose; as Michael R. G. Spiller observes, "While one might casually pen a fourteen-line stanza of three quatrains ending with a couplet, one could not sustain this for [twenty-one] sonnets without recognizing

---

[22] Philip Sidney, *A Defence of Poetry*, ed. J. A. Van Dorsten (Oxford: Oxford Univ. Press, 1966), 22.

[23] Theophile James Meek, "The Structure of Hebrew Poetry," *The Journal of Religion* 9, no. 4 (1929): 523–50, here 533.

[24] Similarities do exist. On occasion Hebrew poetry features the antithetic, a secondary form of parallelism dependent on contrast not entirely unlike a sonnet's turn. See also Deirdre Serjeantson, "The Book of Psalms and the early modern sonnet," *Renaissance Studies* 29, no. 4 (2015): 632–49.

the repetition of the form."[25] Yet even Spiller, an admirer of Lock and adherent of her authorship, questions the intentionality of her choice of form. He posits that the sequence suggests "innocence rather than sophistication" and discussing the single two-sonnet sentence that opens the sequence, asserts that "an experienced sonneteer might try to write a twenty-eight line sentence as a tour de force, but it must at this stage of the sonnet's career in Britain be simple innocence ... that produces this remarkable opening."[26] At a glance, the *Meditation* does seem to lack the key characteristics of sonnets and sonnet sequences. Spiller points to the infrequent breaks at the octave/sestet turn, for example, identifying only nine, while Sarah C. E. Ross notes the "lack of engagement with the technology of the psychological turn" and "reiterative paraphrases."[27]

However, I find that rather than demonstrating innocence, the *Meditation* intentionally draws much of its power from its chosen form, and that rather than remaining static, the sonnets move toward significant resolution.[28] The strict requirements of the sonnet allow the author to reflect at length on each line of the original psalm while maintaining a sensation of stifling isolation, not so unlike Wroth in her labyrinth; as each line of the psalm is transformed into a fourteen-line exploration of the penitent's mind, the characteristic repetition—similar, again, to biblical Hebrew

---

25 Michael R. G. Spiller, "A literary 'first': the sonnet sequence of Anne Locke (1560)," *Renaissance Studies* 11, no. 1 (1997): 45–55, here 48. In addition to the twenty-one sonnets that comprise the *Meditation*'s paraphrase of Psalm 51, the sequence opens with a separate five-sonnet introduction. Hence, Spiller references twenty-six sonnets, not twenty-one.

26 Ibid., 50–51.

27 Sarah C. E. Ross, "Elizabeth Melville and the religious sonnet sequence in Scotland and England," in *Early Modern Women and the Poem*, ed. Susan Wiseman (Manchester: Manchester Univ. Press, 2013), 42–59, here 45–46.

28 Christian Coppa similarly observes that the sequence's "meditative logic of repetition, dilation and recapitulation generates a spiral rather than circular movement," though he does not discuss the role of form. "Supplicating in Agony and Praise: Anne Vaughan Lock and the Case of the Sinner's 'Crye,'" *Religion & Literature* 49, no. 2 (2007): 240–52, here 242.

poetry—serves to draw in the already-tight walls of the sonnet even further. Most importantly, the spiritual sequence still revolves around desire, and Petrarchan glimmerings throughout the poems demonstrate the suitability of the sonnet for the poet's purposes. Though freezing fires or burning cold are not described, at turns the sequence is both aflame and frozen: the contrast between the chill of grief and the warmth of mercy recurs as a metaphor, and the sonneteer draws no shortage of oxymoronic pleasure from her agony, as when she warns of the "bitter frute" of "foule delight" (15.10).[29] Much of the figurative language recalls the Petrarchan impossibility of description, too, as when it describes the "vnperfect shade of perfect lyght" (9.3) or when it takes the psalmist's epithet "whiter than snow" (Ps. 51.7) and magnifies it into a color "whiter than the whitest snowe" (9.14).[30]

At times, the sequence engages even more obviously with the conventions of the sonnet even as it breaks from theological convention, as exemplified by three sonnets near the end of the sequence, the seventeenth through nineteenth sonnets, which I will now discuss. In these three poems, I believe Lock configures God as poetic muse and drawing on this trope as a woman, presents her pain to her divine beloved as a sacrificial offering born from her longing and even desperate hope that divine pity might obtain for her the grace she desires.

Thus, in the seventeenth sonnet, Lock explicitly positions God as both muse and object of her desire. She writes as follows:

Lord, open thou my lippes, and my mouth shal shewe thy praise.[31]
Lo straining crampe of colde despeir againe

---

29 Compare to Petrarch's own *acerbo frutto* (6.13) or *dolci durezze* (351.1). Petrarch, *The Canzoniere*, ed. Mark Musa (Bloomington: Indiana Univ. Press, 1996).

30 Compare Thomas Wyatt's attempts to describe the height of "vnmesurable montayns" (33.1). Thomas Wyatt, *Collected Poems of Sir Thomas Wyatt*, ed. Kenneth Muir (Cambridge, MA: Harvard Univ. Press, 1950).

31 Lock includes an original translation of each of the nineteen verses from Psalm 51 in the margin beside the corresponding sonnet, intentionally presenting the translations alongside her poems. To preserve that

> In feble brest doth pinche my pinyng hart,
> So as in greatest nede to cry and plaine
> My speache doth faile to vtter thee my smart.
> Refreshe my yeldyng hert, with warming grace,
> And loose my speche, and make me call to thee.
> Lord open thou my lippes to shewe my case,
> My Lord, for mercy Loe to thee I flee.
> I can not pray without thy mouyng ayde,
> Ne can I ryse, ne can I stande alone.
> Lord, make me pray, & grant whe I haue praide,
> Lord loose my lippes, I may expresse my mone,
> And findyng grace with open mouth I may
> Thy mercies praise, and holy name display. (17.1–14)

Expanding on the Biblical verse, Lock asks God five times to enable her poetry: "Loose my speche," "make me call to thee," "open thou my lippes," "make me pray," "loose my lippes." As she preserves and at moments intensifies the psalmist's despair, Lock's verse mirrors the parallelism of the psalms; rather than reiterative paraphrase, however, these lines instead suggest a purposeful merging of the psalmist's voice with that of the sonneteer, as Lock calls attention to the role of her divine muse as the one who allows her to speak her despair.

Lock recalls the original parallelism through sound as well, particularly in her distinctive doubled alliteration. For example, the "crampe" and "pinche" of sorrow lead her to "cry and plaine," and "loose ... speche" allows her "lippes to shewe" her case. Internal rhyme, too, amplifies the sense that her "speache doth fail" as the "straining" of the first line carries into "plaine" in the third and "faile" in the fourth. Although Lock extends the psalm, she does so through repetition that reinforces its meaning; her cry of despair sounds deeply familiar even though she does not draw upon the words of the psalmist until the seventh line.

Yet this repetition does not mean that Lock's meaning remains static, and it is in this respect that Lock uses the sonnet to push beyond the original text. The sonnet begins with internal struggle, plunging her reader into the tortured mind of the speaker. But the

---

effect, I first present the verse translation in italics (as quoted in the *Meditation*), followed by the fourteen-line sonnet.

second quatrain introduces movement and renewal, or at least the hope of such: her "pinyng hart" turns "yeldyng," and warm grace eases cold despair. Only then can Lock ask God to "make me call to thee," and this plea succeeds, for in the next line, she at last arrives at the opening words of the original verse and directly addresses the divine. The movement of the sonnet gains an added physicality as Lock describes what she cannot do: she pleads for help to pray, then to rise, and then to stand without aid. The speaker morphs from prostrate sinner to grateful worshipper standing tall in praise. Her requests to God show similar development. She first asks God to make her cry; as she moves towards grace, she asks God to make her pray. In the final poems, moreover, Lock builds towards a crescendo of praise that hardly resembles her first pleas for mercy.

While Lock moves subtly towards resolution in her seventeenth sonnet, the eighteenth sonnet features Lock's sharpest turn, one that divides not only the sonnet but the entire sequence. The infrequency of strong turns throughout the sequence adds power to this transformative shift:

If thou haddest desired sacrifice, I wold haue geuen thou delytest not
    in burnt offringes.
Thy mercies praise, instede of sacrifice,
With thankfull minde so shall I yeld to thee.
For if it were delitefull in thine eyes,
Or hereby mought thy wrath appeased be
Of cattell slayne and burnt with sacred flame
Up to the heauen the vaprie smoke to send:
Of gyltlesse beastes, to purge my gilt and blame,
On altars broylde the sauour shold ascend,
To pease thy wrath. But thy swete sonne alone,
With one sufficing sacrifice for all
Appeaseth thee, and maketh the at one
With sinfull man, and hath repaird our fall.
That sacred hoste is euer in thine eyes.
The praise of that I yeld for sacrifice. (18.1–14)

Although Lock opens the sonnet by claiming praise as an alternative to the sacrifice of cattle on the altar, with the second sentence, beginning in line 3, she paints a vivid image of material offerings that stretches into the ninth line, far exceeding the passing mention of such offerings in the original psalm. As the sentence continues, it seems as if the poet has been consumed by her own imagery: the flames and smoke rising from the burning bodies of "gyltlesse beastes" obscure the mercy of the first line, as does the repeated emphasis on God's wrath. But the oppressive darkness of the sonnet—indeed, of the sequence—is suddenly interrupted by the entrance of "thy swete sonne" in line 9, Lock's most obvious turn. Although Lock almost always follows the English sonnet form (with very slight variations), she frequently divides her thoughts between octave and sestet. The turn here in line 9, however, comes too late for the octave yet several lines too early for a closing couplet, and thus, in and out of time and meter, the *volta* is utterly unexpected yet long awaited, much like Lock's long-awaited introduction of Christ himself. The entire sequence builds towards this pivotal moment.

Like Petrarch's lover, at times Lock's speaker grapples with pain made more painful by its indeterminacy. Infinite sin requires infinite mercy. As the speaker grieves in one of the earlier sonnets, "Ofte hath thy mercie washed me before, / Thou madest me cleane: but I am foule againe" (3.5–6); and she later cries, "Ah wash me, Lord: for I am foule alas" (9.11). But when Christ arrives in the eighteenth sonnet, the sequence begins to recall the distinction between the indeterminate pain of foul sin and the infinite mercy of Christ's unitive love. In what is a remarkable theological move, Lock contrasts the singularity of Christ with the enormity of sin: it is God's "swete sonne alone, / With one sufficing sacrifice for all" who has "repaird our fall." No longer must Lock ask God to cleanse her. The infinite "repair" has been made, and so, with the final words of the eighteenth sonnet, Lock can meet Christ's sacrifice with a sacrifice of her own, a sacrifice of "praise."

In the nineteenth sonnet, the sequence becomes a mutual act of exchange. Lock considers her sacrifice with a catalog of detail:

> *The sacrifice to God is a trobled spirit: a broken and an humbled hart,*
>   *o god, thou wilt not despise.*
> I yeld my self, I offer vp my ghoste,
> My slayne delightes, my dyeng hart to thee.
> To God a trobled sprite is pleasing hoste.
> My trobled sprite doth drede like him to be,
> In whome tastlesse languor with lingring paine
> Hath febled so the starued appetite,

> That foode to late is offred all in vaine,
> To holde in fainting corps the fleing sprite.
> My pining soule for famine of thy grace
> So feares alas the faintnesse of my faithe.
> I offre up my trobled sprite: alas,
> My trobled sprite refuse not in thy wrathe.
> Such offring likes thee, ne wilt thou despise
> The broken humbled hart in angry wise. (19.1–14)

The original psalm does not involve the speaker in the act of sacrifice, offering instead a passive definition. Lock, however, boldly turns the psalm into an active offering of her entire being: her "self," her "ghoste," her "delightes," her "hart," her "sprite." She dismantles herself in front of God, dividing her body into pieces, blazon-like. She submits to the beloved; she yields.

Following upon the extended description of animal sacrifice in the eighteenth sonnet, the image here of the poet-narrator's "dying heart" offered to her God takes on visceral power, as does the sonnet's language of appetite and consumption. The exchange Lock hopes to make with God is not only spiritual, but physical: he must take her heart and, famished, she hungers for his grace. This image of mutual consumption emphasizes the ways in which the sonnet sequence turns God into both muse and lover. Mary Trull observes that throughout the sequence, Lock "places the speaker in a specifically feminine posture in relation to Christ as a lover."[32] Yet David lingers in Trull's reading, as he does for so many: she describes how Lock's "speaker turns *his* eyes to God" (my emphasis added).[33] Certainly, this sequence enables Lock to assume the voice of the psalmist. But instead, Lock emphasizes the feminine position of the speaker in a psalm where the speaker is otherwise entirely ungendered. While many psalms (including two of the six other Penitential Psalms) give the gender of the speaker within the text of the psalm itself, only an initial attribution to David genders

---

[32] Mary Trull, "Petrarchism and the Gift: The Sacrifice of Praise in Anne Lock's 'A Meditation of a Penitent Sinner,'" *Religion & Literature* 41, no. 3 (2009): 1–25, here 18.

[33] Ibid.," 21. Hannay similarly describes Lock's use of "the male persona of the psalmist king" ("Unlock My Lipps,'" 35).

Psalm 51. Lock chooses to translate a psalm where she can speak in her own voice.

Praise upon the Altar

One final thread ties the seventeenth through nineteenth sonnets together. Perhaps most remarkably, when read in sequence, they begin to resemble something very much like a fragment of a corona. While Lock does not repeat lines exactly, she does repeat phrases; the first and last lines of the three sonnets clearly echo one another, even as their meaning shifts. The seventeenth sonnet ends with tentative hope: "I may / Thy mercies praise, and holy name display" (17.13–14). In the next line of the sequence, the eighteenth sonnet turns that possibility into reality: "Thy mercies praise, instead of sacrifice, / With thankfull minde so shall I yeld to thee" (18.1–2). The sonnet concludes with "the praise of that I yeld for sacrifice" (18.14), while the nineteenth sonnet begins by explaining precisely what it is Lock plans to yield: "I yeld my self" (19.1). This linear development suggests that Lock did not simply intend to write one long poem or a score of fourteen-line poems but a true sonnet sequence, following one path from beginning to end. The *Meditation* thus begins to anticipate a sequence like John Donne's "La Corona," with its keen awareness of the immensity of a little room and its spiraling movement towards ascension.[34]

In the end, Lock finds herself in a space quite different from that where she began: the last sonnet of the sequence features one final striking deviation from her source. The original psalm concludes as worshippers insist on physical sacrifice, presenting "burnt offering and oblation ... [and] calves upon thine altar" (Ps. 51.19). But Lock's sacrifice differs. Instead, she writes, "Thou shalt behold vpon thine altar lye / Many a yelden host of humbled hart, / And

---

34 For more on the form and movement of "La Corona," see Margaret Maurer, "The Circular Argument of Donne's 'La Corona,'" *Studies in English Literature, 1500–1900* 22, no. 1 (1982): 51–68. Also much like the *Meditation*, Donne's final offering is his own creation of prayer and praise. Closer consideration of the *Meditation* as a predecessor of later sequences like "La Corona" may be one promising path for further study.

round about then shall thy people crye: / We praise thee, God our God" (21.5–8). She turns to God and requests mercy one last time, so that she "may also honor thee" (21.10). Rather than an image of burnt offerings, she concludes with an offering of heart and song. With her carefully crafted poems, Lock adds her voice to the chorus; she proudly sets her praise upon the altar. In perhaps the very first English sonnet sequence, a woman tells a story that moves from silence to speech, and in doing so, justifies the worth of her own words as sacred offering.

Appendix: Psalm 51 as found in the Geneva Bible (1560)[35]

To him that excelleth, A psalme of David, when the Prophet Nathan came unto him, after he had gone in to Beth-sheba.

1 Have mercie upon me, o God, according to thy loving kindness: according to the multitude of thy compassions put away mine iniquities.

2 Wash me thoroughly from mine iniquitie, and cleanse me from my sin.

3 For I know mine iniquities, and my sin *is* ever before me.

4 Against thee, against thee only have I sinned, and done evil in thy sight, that thou maiest be just when thou speakest, *and* pure when thou judgest.

5 Behold, I was born in iniquity, and in sin hath my mother conceived me.

6 Behold, thou lovest truth in the inward affections: therefore hast thou taught me wisdom in the secret of *mine heart.*

7 Purge me with hyssop, and I shal be clean: wash me, and I shalbe whiter than snow.

8 Make me to hear joy and gladnes, *that* the bones, *which* thou hast broken, may rejoice.

9 Hide thy face from my sins, and put away all mine iniquities.

---

[35] *Geneva Bible 1560,* The Psalms of David, accessed May 23, 2024, http://www.genevabible1560.com/pdf/Old%20Testament/Psalms.pdf.

10 Create in me a cleane heart, o God, and renue a right spirit within me.

11 Cast me not awaie from thy presence, and take not thine holie Spirit from me.

12 Restore to me the joy of thy salvation, and stablish me with *thy* free Spirit.

13 *Then* shal I teach thy ways unto the wicked, and sinners shal be converted unto thee.

14 Deliver me from blood, o God, *which art* the God of my salvation, *and* my tongue shal sing joyfully of thy righteousness.

15 Open thou my lips, o Lord, and my mouth shal shewe forth thy praise.

16 For thou desirest no sacrifice, though I would give it: thou delitest not in burnt offering.

17 The sacrifices of God *are* a contrite spirit: a contrite and a broke heart, o God, thou wilt not despise.

18 Be favorable unto Zion for thy good pleasure: build the walls of Jerusalem.

19 Then shal thou accept the sacrifices of righteousness, *even* the burnt offering and oblation: then shal they offer calves upon thine altar.

University of Virginia

Renaissance Utopia as Deliberative Monologue: Andrzej Frycz Modrzewski and Thomas More

Václav Zheng

Modern utopian studies owe a great debt to Thomas More, who not only coined the term "utopia," a pun meaning "good/no place," but also published in 1516 the book *Utopia* which left much mystery for later readers and critics. In this classic work, we encounter a straightforward monologic description of life on the utopian islands (Book 2), preceded (or, chronologically, followed) by a rather ambiguous dialogue that provides context and pretext for the utopian adventure (Book 1). Using classical rhetorical categories, Book 2 introduces the travel account in the manner of the epidiectic rhetoric of praise while Book 1 adopts the deliberative rhetoric of political advice.[1]

From this prototypical model, scholars have readily produced an inventory of utopian constructions and incorporated similar fictions

---

1 Literary scholarship on Thomas More is both bountiful and diverse, and discussion on the rhetorical and formal strategies in his *Utopia* reached its peak in the 1980s. For a recent summary, see Elizabeth McCutcheon, "More's Rhetoric," in *The Cambridge Companion to Thomas More*, ed. George M. Logan (Cambridge: Cambridge Univ. Press, 2011): 54–57. Ancient rhetorical theory (Aristotle, Cicero, and Quintilian) recognizes three *genera*: judicial/forensic (legal controversy), demonstrative/epidiectic (praise or blame), and deliberative (policy and persuasion). Judicial lost its leading role in the Renaissance, so it is excluded from our further discussion. See John F. Tinkler, "Renaissance Humanism and the genera eloquentiae," *Rhetorica* 5, no. 3 (1987): 281–86.

into the utopian canon, thereby inventing a self-contained literary genre.[2] Some works closely resemble More's Book 2 in form such as Johann Valentin Andreae's *Christianopolis* (1619) and Francis Godwin's *The Man in the Moone* (1638), and others blend the rhetorical mode of Book 2 with the speech style of Book 1 as seen in Tommaso Campanella's *The City of the Sun* (1602/1623) and Francis Bacon's *New Atlantis* (1627). In recent years, a group of English literary critics, represented by Nina Chordas, Chloë Houston, and Sarah Hogan, has sought to identify dialogue as a defining form of early modern utopia and to subsume utopian literature under the umbrella of travel writing and ethnography. They maintain that these genres share similar narrative structures and literary themes: Fictional characters recount their experiences in a remotely located ideal society through conversation. This scholarly approach not only aligns with the spatial and narrative template of Thomas More but also reflects the emerging imperial mentality of sixteenth- and seventeenth-century Western Europeans.[3]

But we may raise the question: Is early modern utopian writing truly a cohesive genre in motif and form? This essay challenges the canons and boundaries of Renaissance utopian literature from rhetorical and poetic perspectives by introducing a sixteenth-century Polish utopian text written in Latin, *De Republica emendanda* (*On the Improvement of the Republic*) by Andrzej Frycz Modrzewski

---

2   Much of this happened during and after the 1970s which indicated a growing scholarly interest in utopianism. Of particular significance, Darko Suvin reconfigured utopia as a literary genre of cognitive estrangement subordinated by science fiction. See Darko Suvin, "Defining the Literary Genre of Utopia: Some Historical Semantics, some Genealogy, a Proposal and a Plea," *Studies in the Literary Imagination* 6, no. 2 (1973): 121–45. Another influential precursor was Robert C. Elliott, author of *The Shape of Utopia: Studies in a Literary Genre* (Chicago: Univ. of Chicago Press, 1970). Additionally, the Society for Utopian Studies (1975–) was founded around the same time.

3   The major works referred here include Nina Chordas, *Forms in Early Modern Utopia: The Ethnography of Perfection* (Aldershot and Burlington, VT: Ashgate, 2013), Chloë Houston, *The Renaissance Utopia: Dialogue, Travel and the Ideal Society* (Farnham: Ashgate, 2014), and Sarah Hogan, *Other Englands: Utopia, Capital, and Empire in an Age of Transition* (Stanford, CA: Stanford Univ. Press, 2018).

(1503–72).[4] I argue that the speech mode found in this political treatise, deliberative monologue, presents a distinct kind of early modern utopia and conveys a no less powerful sense of utopian yearning than Thomas More's *Utopia* or any other utopian works that use rhetorical forms besides deliberative monologue: deliberative dialogue, demonstrative dialogue, or demonstrative monologue. As a result, this essay advocates for the adoption of a new library of utopian literature that does not necessarily reproduce the Morean archetype.

Andrzej Frycz Modrzewski (or Andrzej Frycz of Modrzew) was born in 1503 to an impoverished noble family from a small town called Wolbórz in Greater Poland (*Wielkopolska*).[5] He moved to Kazimierz for further parish education in 1514 and then studied philosophy at the University of Kraków, where he received a classical humanist education. He then worked at the court of the Polish Primate before traveling abroad in 1531, to Germany, France, and Switzerland. He met Martin Luther in Wittenberg and became a close friend of Philip Melanchthon, from whom he absorbed the ideas of the Protestant Reformation. Back in Poland, he participated in *Sejms* (national meetings) and was appointed as a royal secretary of the Polish Jagiellonian King Sigismund the Old in 1547.

Modrzewski's engagement with government and church made him aware of the social ills of the Polish society, so he decided to devote himself to defending the underprivileged classes and striving for social justice and equality. The first work he drafted and circulated during the 1543 national assembly was named *Mercy, or On the Punishment for Murder* (*Lascius, sive de poena homicidii*). In this pamphlet, Modrzewski advocated that everyone, rich or poor, be equal before the law, share the same rights of life, and face identical

---

4 Marlana Portolano rightly identifies the importance of rhetoric in utopian studies within the liberal-humanist tradition, but her overview of ancient rhetorical theory is rough and her treatment on the Renaissance period is absent. See Marlana Portolano, "The Rhetorical Function of Utopia: An Exploration of the Concept of Utopia in Rhetorical Theory," *Utopian Studies* 23, no. 1 (2012): 113–41.

5 For an erudite albeit old biography of Modrzewski, see Stanisław Kot, *Andrzej Frycz Modrzewski: studjum a dziejów kultury polskiej w. XVI* (Kraków: Nakł. Akademii Umiejętności, 1919).

punishment when committing crimes regardless of social status; Modrzewski believed no exemption or sentence reduction should be granted even if a nobleman killed a plebeian, a point the French scholar Jean Bodin considered "absurd."[6] In 1545, Modrzewski presented a speech to protect the interests of townspeople who were prohibited from buying landed goods from the noble lords. Modrzewski published his magnum opus, *De Republica emendanda*, in Basel in 1554. This work not only incorporates ancient Greek and Roman authors like Aristotle, Cicero, and Polybius, but also borrows ideas from contemporary writers such as Erasmus, Luther, Calvin, and Juan Luis Vives, as Polish historians have observed.[7]

In comparison to More's *Utopia*, Modrzewski's *De Republica emendanda* is not a utopian fiction in any conventional sense. It lacks the theatrical characters, narrative plots, exotic journeys, distant islands, and fictionally "real" exotic inhabitants typically associated with the genre; it neither contains a single line of literary travelogue nor does it contain any dramatic dialogue. Instead, the work belongs to a different category of writing and embodies a political, if not philosophical treatise, that Modrzewski, as royal counselor and a humanist, submitted to the young Polish king Sigismund August around 1550 with the objective of reforming the state.

It is essential to state upfront that *De Republica emendanda* was not intended as a satire but as a social commentary and genuine petition circulated in the highest political spheres. It was widely known, read, and contested in the mid-sixteenth century, both within Poland and across Europe. Modrzewski was an advocate of social justice at the Polish national meetings, and a surviving letter testifies that he once entreated King Sigismund to accept his advice

---

6 Jean Bodin, *De Republica libri sex* (Lyon, 1586), 762: "quod nihil absurdius ab eo scribi potuit, qui suae Republicae leges ac mores conformare vellet."

7 For example, Stanisław Kot, *Wpływ starożytności klasycznej na teorye polityczne Andrzeja Frycza z Modrzewa* (Kraków: Nakł. Akademii umiejętności, 1911) and Jan Twardowski, *Jan Ludwik Vives i Andrzej Frycz Modrzewski* (Kraków: PAU, 1921). Later Polish historians, or Fryczologists, focused mostly on its sociopolitical thought rather than its utopian qualities and formal schemes. See Waldemar Voisé, *Frycza Modrzewskiego Nauka o Państwie i Prawie* (Warsaw: Książka i Wiedza, 1956).

for social improvement.⁸ He also had no reason or motivation to deceive the king with his radical—even dangerous—undertaking, especially considering the hostility he faced from conservative Polish magnates and powerful church leaders who later not only censored his publication but also caused him great suffering. Nonetheless, Modrzewski's masterpiece maintains a significant utopian element because while striving to improve contemporary Polish society, the work apparently seeks a perfect, meritocratic Poland that neither existed at the time nor seemed possible to realize in the future.⁹

Modrzewski's rhetorical strategy of deliberative monologue remains consistent throughout his text. *De Republica emendanda* originally consisted of five books: (1) *On Custom* (*De Moribus*); (2) *On Law* (*De Legibus*); (3) *On War* (*De Bello*); (4) *On Church* (*De Ecclesia*); and (5) *On School* (*De Schola*). Each book is further divided into sections in which Modrzewski expounds aspects of the ideal commonwealth through argumentation using classical thought and historical examples. For instance, the first section of Book 1 is titled "A Definition of Republic" (*Republicae definitio*) where Modrzewski draws on Aristotelian teaching to explain what constitutes a good republic:¹⁰ "A republic consists of assemblies of people, gathered together from various neighborhoods and determined to lead a good and happy life." In the second section, "The Division of Republic" (*Reipublicae diuisio*), he again follows Aristotle in differentiating between monarchy and tyranny, aristocracy and oligarchy, and democracy and anarchy. He proposes a mixed government as the best solution, arguing that, where "the king rules everything,

---

8 Andrzej Frycz Modrzewski, *Opera Omnia*, Vol. 1 (Kraków: PIW, 1953), 553–54.

9 Compared to Thomas More, scholarship on Modrzewski is much thinner, and most of them have viewed *De Republica emendanda* as a work of political thought only. Nonetheless, there have been some previous Polish and continental debates, both agreements and disagreements, regarding its utopian qualities. For instance, see Waldemar Voisé, *Frycza Modrzewskiego nauka o państwie I prawie* (Warsaw: Książka i Wiedza, 1956), 300–302 and Claude Backvis, "Le courant utopique dans la Pologne de la Renaissance," in *Les Utopies à La Renaissance: Colloque International* (Brussels: Presses univ. de Bruxelles, 1963), 163–208.

10 Modrzewski, *Opera Omnia*, Vol. 1, 30–33.

nobleman are given more important offices, and everyone is allowed to claim fame from acts of valor." Clearly, what Modrzewski presents is by no means a physical description of a given place like Thomas More presents in Book 2 of *Utopia*, but rather a theoretical clarification of how an ideal state should operate and why it is superior to other possibilities.[11]

It might be helpful to pause and review the difference between the two classical oratory genera called by Aristotle the *epideictic* and *deliberative*. The epideictic division of oratory, a popular rhetorical practice among Renaissance humanists, is commonly used to extol or condemn a person or a place during ceremonial occasions. It was particularly prevalent in the fifteenth century in the literary genre of city encomia, that is, speeches praising a city or commonwealth. According to Cicero, epideictic rhetoric involves three standard *topoi* or commonplaces: *corpus* ("physical attributes"), *res externae* ("external circumstances"), *animus* ("qualities of character or virtue"), and the first two can be combined into one overarching topoi named *fortuna* ("fortune"). Therefore, epideictic oratory in general deals with moral conformity and incongruity between external fortune and internal virtue in relation to the vicissitudes of a man or a city, and is often depicted through hyperbolic evocation.[12] This is roughly how Thomas More portrays and celebrates the ideal commonwealth via Raphael Hythloday in Book 2 of *Utopia*.

In contrast, the deliberative style is commonly related to policy making and political persuasion with the topoi of *honestas* ("honorability"), *utilitas* ("expediency"), and *necessitas* ("necessity"). As a rhetoric aimed at an uncertain future, it juggles what is morally right and what is realistically beneficial in guiding governmental decisions.[13] A classic Renaissance example is *Il principe* (1513/1532). With a clear political end, Niccolò Machiavelli openly pronounces his pragmatic tactics of statesmanship and advises young princes to take advantage of necessary actions to gain and maintain power

---

11 Cf. Thomas More, *Utopia*, eds. Clarence H. Miller, George M. Logan, and Robert M. Adams (Cambridge: Cambridge Univ. Press, 1995), 108–11.

12 Cicero, *Rhetorica ad Herennium: Book 3* (Cambridge, MA: Harvard Univ. Press 2014), 172–84.

13 Ibid., 156–72.

in order to strengthen the Florentine Republic.[14] Another example comes in *Utopia*'s Book 1, which, according to George Logan, exemplifies a deliberative debate where the three characters share their political opinions and seek harmony and compromise concerning the topoi of honor and expediency.[15] So it would seem natural that Modrzewski utilizes the deliberative mode to suggest practical political advice for the Polish king. But while such advice is supposed to embody realism and utilitarianism, I would like to address why Modrzewski should be considered a utopian thinker from a rhetorical perspective.

As evidence for my hypothesis, I will focus on the ways in which Modrzewski employs the deliberative rhetorical approach in discussing the education of children in Section 6 of Book 1. After proclaiming the importance of individual virtue for societal wellbeing, Modrzewski, as narrator-cum-lawgiver, proceeds to discuss the importance of parents in instilling good manners in children and preparing them for a virtuous and prudent life. The author highlights childhood as a pivotal stage in moral development because whatever people learn and get accustomed to in youth, whether good or bad, stays with them for their entire life. To illustrate this point, Modrzewski offers a metaphor comparing mankind to plants. He says: "If you give a seedling venom, when it then grows into a large tree, the fruit that comes from it will harm those who eat it and will also cause great harm to the seed."[16] Furthermore, to persuade parents to take due responsibility, Modrzewski remarks that Christ loves to take great care of children, while warning that God will punish those who ill-treat a youngster by "hanging millstones around their necks and drowning them in the sea." After stressing the basic principles, Modrzewski outlines for Polish parents a "practical" protocol for the diligent training of youth. This includes feeding children but not in excess, commending virtues through examples, forbidding laziness and idleness, separating boys

---

14 See Virginia Cox, "Machiavelli and the *Rhetorica ad Herennium*: Deliberative Rhetoric in The Prince," *The Sixteenth Century Journal* 28, no. 4 (1997): 1109–41.
15 George M. Logan, "Utopia and Deliberative Rhetoric," *Moreana* 31, nos. 2–3 (1994): 103–20.
16 Modrzewski, *Opera Omnia*, Vol. 1, 43–48.

from girls (to inhibit carnal lust), prohibiting brutal and dangerous games, and precluding childhood association with evils like pleasure, obscenity, anger, violence, and luxury. Most importantly, Modrzewski admonishes parents to practice virtues themselves in their everyday behavior so they can serve as role models for their sons and daughters. He discourages parents from impropriety, admonishing, for example, that "a drunken father will not be able to make his son love sobriety."

Similar childrearing themes also exist in Thomas More's "textual construction" of the utopian society. In Book 2 of *Utopia*, the narrator Hythloday mentions in several different places familial dynamics and parental education.[17] For instance, Utopian residents adhere to the custom of seniority in communal life, where children are essentially considered servants of their parents, just as wives were servants of their husbands. Hence, during every "Last Feast," children kneel before their parents and confess their sins, and it is the parents themselves who scold and punish their sons and daughters for minor transgressions without the need for any public recriminations. Nonetheless, children on the utopian islands also enjoy certain privileges of childhood, such as playing with gems. When parents find beautiful gems, they "polish them and give them as decorations to the children," who in turn "feel proud and pleased." As their young minds mature, the children voluntarily put away these toys without being asked to do so by their parents, about which the narrator comments, saying the following: "Just as our children when they grow up, put away their marbles, baubles and dolls."

Noticeably, in the practice of epideictic rhetoric, More—through the mouth of Hythloday—vividly depicts everyday life on the remote utopian island. His narrative not only records physical actions (kneeling down) and family anecdotes (the gem story) but also reveals certain social norms and conventions (e.g., children as servants and parental responsibilities), gathered through personal observation and local testimony: This is how the society of Utopia has functioned probably for centuries without palpable transformation. This is also why, in terms of diction, Hythloday's account is presented in the third-person present indicative, illustrating the current state of the utopian lifestyles. Hythloday says, for instance,

---

17 More, *Utopia*, 135, 151, 193, 237.

"They [the parents] adorn infants with these [gems]" and "they [the children] confess that they have sinned."[18] Moreover, the narrative also precisely exposes some resemblance but also difference between "our" world and "their" world, as if readers are watching ethnographic footage of an outlandish, though laudable, idealistic commonwealth. John Tinkler remarks that through fiction and hyperbole, More creates a "tangible imago" and a "picture-cum-simile" that is vivid enough to verge on being actually real, whereas its utopian nature lies exactly in a perfect union of true, unchanging human virtues and nonexistent "fortunes," that is—in terms of the topoi of epideictic rhetoric—nonexistent physical attributes and external circumstances.[19]

However, Modrzewski marks a stark contrast with More when it comes to rhetorical presentation because he is using deliberative, and not epideictic, rhetoric. In *De Republica emendanda*, there is no imagined pre-existing society to be revealed by his pen, and no vibrant family life to be witnessed. If one were to pinpoint Modrzewski's ideal society, it must be located in the Kingdom of Poland, but definitely not his contemporary Polish kingdom. His ideal society might take place in the future or even within a timeless space, but his discourse symbolizes his own internal reasoning and rationalization for an ideal Polish state, not a mental drawing and construction. Notably, the visually indefinite and materially indeterminate location of his narrative is reinforced by his choice of grammar and diction. Thus, he chooses to use the subjunctive mood countless times in his writing. Just to take a few examples, he says the following: "Let parents then be diligent in training their sons [*Curent igitur parentes filios suos iis institutis et praeceptis erudiri*]"; "May they forbid them (children) from acquaintance of evil men [*hominum malorum consuetudine eis interdicant*]"; and "Let them hinder them from impropriety of words [*uerborum improbitate eos cohibeant*]."[20] These jussive expressions, in contrast to the *Utopia*'s present indicative, reflect Modrzewski's perception of, and perhaps confidence in,

---

18 More, *Utopia*, 150, 236.
19 John F. Tinkler, "Praise and Advice: Rhetorical Approaches in More's *Utopia* and Machiavelli's *The Prince*," *The Sixteenth Century Journal* 19, no. 2 (1988): 187–207.
20 Modrzewski, *Opera Omnia*, Vol. 1, 43–44.

the possible realization of his ideal society if his protocols are only followed. Nevertheless, he does not offer a concrete drawing of the ideal commonwealth as More does; instead, Modrzewski merely glances afar and steers people, deliberating upon an honorable path that he believes can ideally lead to ultimate fulfillment.

In his deliberations, Modrzewski puts almost all his weight on the deliberative *topoi* of honorability (*honestas*) and fails to take expediency (*utilitas*) or necessity (*necessitas*) into serious consideration. In other words, he spills so much ink on the pursuit of an ideal that pragmatic matters remain unresolved. Practical questions arise: For example, if Polish children are to be taught moral goodness by their parents, who teaches the parents themselves if they are already "contaminated" by their environment or even by their own parents? There seems to be a need for a mechanism to ensure that adults are in fact moral exemplars for their children. But none is given. Furthermore, it could take several generations, if not forever, to see the maturation of such an ideal society. Modrzewski never specifies how moral behavior is to be instituted among adults in the first place. What seems even more curious, given the function of his text as a proposal for the Polish king, is that Modrzewski does not address the question of how he expects the king to enforce his decrees and effect general compliance. Therefore, unlike Machiavelli who also uses the deliberative mode, Modrzewski offers no expedient tactics for royal administrative oversight. He points his fellow Poles towards a road of total reform while providing few practical means to get there. For this very reason, Modrzewski's use of classical deliberative rhetoric causes a utopian paradox, a split between the radicality of his ambitions and the impracticality of his proposals.

The utopian absurdity emanating from Modrzewski's deliberative rhetoric is further accentuated by his monologic frankness. Since Modrzewski employs no fictitious dialogue or imaginary conversation in his entire work, he writes as a solitary commentator, expressing a personal hope that his ideas will be heard by an audience equally eager to change the status quo. He is not only the author of the work but also the narrator of the treatise and even the lawgiver of the proposed improvements for the Polish Commonwealth. Thus, in the section on parental education, we find several occasions where Modrzewski asserts his narratorial authority while delivering his argument. For example, when discussing precautions against game playing that children must abide by, he writes, "As I have said [*ut dixi*], let all games be honest"; likewise, when mentioning the damage that moral corruption can cause, he again uses the phrase "as I have said" (*ut dixi*). Moreover, when asking parents to reflect on their own habits and their possible impact on the habits of their children, he proclaims, "Here I wish that each parent would look at themselves [*hic uelim unusquisque parentum se inspiciat*]."[21] Such self-referential language focusing on the first-person *I* abounds throughout the work, repeatedly reminding us of Modrzewski's personal stake in his idealistic project.

Because they reflect Modrzewski's own voice, these frequent first-person intrusions carry multiple rhetorical implications. First, without any narrative restraint or plot structure, Modrzewski can run through his ideas freely and call upon whomever he is concerned with at any given moment: children, parents, the king, the general readership, and at times, even himself as if he is speaking aloud into the face of a timeless void. He levels his audience as if all readers are one and the same—with him. Second, he does not conceal, but rather he foregrounds his visions and viewpoints, willingly bringing all he has in his mind to light. This authorial presence centers Modrzewski as the one who is most liable for bringing about the ideal state. Third, although devoid of conversation or debate conducted by multiple characters, Modrzewski's monologic text is still able to coerce readers to listen to and consider his personal opinions about what he believes is morally correct. The effect of this monologic approach, in contrast to a textual dialogism that promotes multivocality, equality, and inclusion, is that it elevates Modrzewski's own power of voice as he is the central and sole actor in a discourse that cannot anticipate—nor even allow—any response or opposition from "interlocutors" residing outside the text.[22] If

---

21 Modrzewski, *Opera Omnia*, Vol. 1, 46–48.
22 There is far more Renaissance scholarship on dialogism than monologism. We must borrow the oft-quoted words of Bakhtin: "The monologue is finalized and deaf to the other's response, does not expect it and does not acknowledge it in any decisive force. Monologue manages without the other, and therefore to some degree materializes all reality. Monologue pretends to be the ultimate word. It closes down the represented

Modrzewski is creating an "imago" through his monologue, it is a lucid image of his own inner, even zealous, ruminations and utopian dreams rather than an animated picture of a happy utopian land existing somewhere out there in the external world.

Compared to Modrzewski's presentation of his own real thoughts, Thomas More remains a rather cryptic figure. Nowhere in Book 2 of *Utopia* do we find him exposing his identity or real attitudes, except in the title which credits him as the transcriber of Hythloday's account: "per Thomam Morum."[23] Scholars have long debated whether More is a playful satirist or a truthful philosopher. This debate ends like a myth, if not an interdisciplinary wrangling, sundered between, on one side, literary critics who painstakingly seek to grasp More's humanist intention behind the literary veil, and on the other side, political theorists who uncritically report upon his intellectual debt and social criticism.[24] But one thing people can agree on is that the dialogic nature of the often-neglected first book of *Utopia* complicates the reception and interpretation of the "plain" utopian description of the second book, which was allegedly composed first.[25] More chooses the Platonic dialogic model and

---

world and represented persons." Mikhail Bakhtin, *Problems of Dostoevsky's Poetics* (Minneapolis: Univ. of Minnesota Press, 1984), 293.

23 More, *Utopia*, 108.

24 Recent attempts include, for the former camp, Bernd Renner, "'Real versus Ideal': Utopia and the Early Modern Satirical Tradition," *Renaissance and Reformation/Renaissance et Réforme* 41, no. 3 (2018): 47–66; and, for the latter, Lawrence Wilde, *Thomas More's Utopia: Arguing for Social Justice* (New York: Taylor & Francis, 2016).

25 For a reconstruction of the sequence of More's writing, see J. H. Hexter, *More's Utopia: The Biography of an Idea* (Princeton, NJ: Princeton Univ. Press, 1952). There are also interpretations that read Book 2 of *Utopia* as more dramatic than a monologue if not a one-sided, ongoing dialogue connected with Book 1. See Andrew M. McLean, "Thomas More's *Utopia* as Dialogue and City Encomium," in *Acta Conventus Neo-Latini Guelpherbytani: Proceedings of the Sixth International Congress of Neo-Latin Studies*, ed. Stella P. Revard, Fidel Radie, and Mario A. Di Cesare (Binghamton, NY: Center for Medieval and Early Renaissance Studies, 1988), 91–97. Also see Richard J. Schoeck, "'A Nursery of Correct and Useful Institutions': On Reading More's *Utopia* as Dialogue," *Moreana* 6, no. 2 (1969): 19–32.

decides to insert himself as a semi-fictional character conversing with the equally semi-fictional Peter Giles and the entirely fictional Hythloday. It is not clear at all, however, which character represents the real thoughts of Sir Thomas More. Irony intersects with honesty in a jocoserious way. The historical More lurks in the dark, quietly chuckling at the two-part sandcastle he has crafted, whispering always that a good place is no place.

Modrzewski is much more simple-minded (or headstrong) than Thomas More. In his deliberative monologue, he pours out his heart and does not hold back his thoughts. However, his reform program was radical and tantamount to pointless, for the common mindset of sixteenth-century Poles. He had too high expectations for human virtue and envisaged too fundamental a change in sociopolitical institutions. Few, especially among the Polish gentry, would have supported him or found his project practical. Without any fictional pretense, he tries, maybe too hard, to have his ideas accepted. Unlike More who hides behind a wall while his interlocutors dance between the real and the ideal, Modrzewski shows no desire to play any word or mind games on behalf of his peers among the literati. Perhaps as a result, his *emendanda* are pessimistic in tone.

Let me bring forth another comparison from Renaissance Italy, Francesco Patrizi and his *Happy City* (*La città felice*, 1553). This concise, dry "utopian" treatise is also set in the monologic mode, with no characters, dialogues, or narrative plots. It accounts the ideal organization and population of an imagined city and to a great extent resembles *Utopia*'s Book 2 in form. Critics have offered various readings of this peculiar work, but narratively, what is different from Modrzewski is that Patrizi offers many fewer first-person intrusions of the singular *I* (*io, sono, me*).[26] When he uses them, it is always in a peaceful and meditative tone.[27] He actually speaks more often in

---

26 Antonio Donato, "An Introduction to The Happy City by Francesco Patrizi of Cherso," in *Italian Renaissance Utopias: Doni, Patrizi, and Zuccolo*, ed. and trans. Antonio Donato (New York: Springer, 2019), 63–73, here 65–66.

27 As an example: "Therefore, I resolved to show, to those who are awake and have the desire to follow me, how to rediscover this river and build a city upon which such a river would continuously fall, washing it with its most happy waters [Mi sono deliberato di voler mostrare, à quelli

the welcoming voice of the first-person plural (*noi, siamo, ce*) as if acting as a tour guide or a city designer. Patrizi is planning out and showing people around the best image of his ideal city in a creative game of imagination. In the conclusion, he states that "if our city is just as we have described it, we will be able to quench our thirst and satiate ourselves most abundantly with the waters that will fall onto it from the blessed whirlpool."[28] It is a wishful and whimsical hope, in contrast to the unbending persistence of Modrzewski.

Modrzewski's sense of pessimism does not spring from the unattainability of his ideal society but from his misconceptions and misunderstandings about utopian impossibility; a utopia is, after all, "no place." Modrzewski's rhetorical use of deliberative monologue exacerbates his farcicality and embroils him in a joke, not a joke as some utopist-satirists propose to their readers, but Modrzewski becomes the object of laughter himself. Ironically, this ridicule may make him a more authentic and idealistic utopist because he never fully comprehends his own absurdity.

Let us return to our original question: is early modern utopia a matter of generic form? Yes and no. No, because, as I would urge, utopian literature is *not* necessarily bound to a specific rhetorical genus, nor intrinsically associated with any particular narrative motif. It instead symbolizes the ardent human impulse towards a perfect world, the craving for a better life, or in Ruth Levitas's words, "the education of desire."[29] It can take diverse modes of representation, whether through text or manifested in the real world, from Renaissance ideal city planning to intentional religious communities. Nonetheless, the formal quality does indeed matter in the way that certain rhetorical styles carry substantial authorial weight and are able to determine the articulation of utopian ideals, as we have shown in Modrzewski's case. The more Modrzewski pushes and appears sincere in his deliberative monologue, the less realistic—and thus more utopian—he seems to become. Perhaps,

---

che haueranno occhio voglia di feguitarmi]." Francesco Patrizi, *The Happy City*, in *Italian Renaissance Utopias*, ed. and trans. Donato, 75–120, here 78.
    28 Ibid., 96.
    29 Ruth Levitas, *The Concept of Utopia* (New York: Peter Lang, 2010), 6.

the boundary of early modern utopia should be expanded and reimagined, from a "game of mind" to a "claim by the blind." In this sense, Thomas More was a light-hearted realist, but Andrzej Frycz Modrzewski was a full-blown utopian.

Johns Hopkins University

Alonso Berruguete's Workshop and the Place of Polychrome Sculpture in the Hierarchy of Arts in Spain

Ilenia Colón Mendoza

THE monumental catalogue of the city of Valladolid alone has over a thousand works inventoried.[1] The city of Valladolid and its surrounding region provided an ideal environment for the flourishing of artists, thanks to its status as the capital of the Spanish Monarchy and its strategic location at the crossroads of commerce during the early modern period. Maria Bolaños, director of the *Museo Nacional de Escultura*, aptly describes the city as a dynamic, cosmopolitan, and innovative artistic laboratory.[2] This vibrant artistic environment, coupled with the support of workshops that promoted artistic collaboration, was instrumental in the production of polychrome sculpture. The sculpture workshops of Valladolid were tight-knit communities that included familial relationships that strengthened production and technical practices. Alonso Berruguete's workshop, in particular, stands out as a unique model for understanding sixteenth-century workshop practices, showcasing his remarkable transition from painter to sculptor. Berruguete's influence extended far beyond his students and followers, shaping sculptural types and influential trends well into the late seventeenth century.

---

1 Esteban García Chico, *Catálogo Monumental de Valladolid*, vols. 1–5 (Valladolid: Diputación Provincial de Valladolid, 1991).

2 *Cuerpos de Dolor: La imagen de lo sagrado en la escultura española 1500–1750: Museo de Bellas Artes de Sevilla, 3 mayo–16 septiembre 2012* (Andalucía: Junta de Andalucía, 2012), 14.

Spain's production of polychrome sculptures in the sixteenth and seventeenth centuries surpassed that of Italy and Flanders. When we consider all the *retablos* and *sillería* (choirstalls), including those made in the Americas, polychrome sculpture emerges as a definitive cornerstone of Spanish Art. Exhibitions like the *Like Life: Sculpture, Color, and the Body*, held at the MET Breuer, underscore polychrome sculpture's significance beyond the realm of specialist scholarship. The exhibition catalogue, for instance, highlights Philip II's request for a bronze sculpture with *encarnaciones* (flesh-colored tones) for the face and hands, underscoring the medium's importance. To fully grasp polychrome sculpture, we must delve into the materiality of wood, the *paragone* (or, in Spanish, *parangón*) as it appears in sculpture and painting treatises, and primary source documents that reveal a workshop organization that was collaborative and highly specialized.

Materiality and the *Parangón*

In the article "Pacheco's *Art of Painting*: The *Parangón* and the Techniques of Spanish Seventeenth-Century Polychrome Sculpture," I discuss the unique status of polychrome sculpture.[3] Within the hierarchy of the arts in Spain, uncolored sculpture is ranked above other sculptures because polychromy elevates them closer to painting. In addition to using polychromy, the choice of wood as a medium is deliberate. Spanish sculptors chose it due to its materiality and sacred associations, as well as its low cost and abundance.[4] In Spain, polychrome wood is used almost exclusively in religious art, effectively creating a "canon" of preference for the material. Christina Neilson notes "that wood was preferred for certain subjects because it was considered a living material that operated like

---

3 Ilenia Colón Mendoza, "Pacheco's *Art of Painting*: The *Parangón* and the Techniques of Spanish Seventeenth-Century Polychrome Sculpture," in *Polychrome Art in Early Modern World 1200–1800*, ed. Ilenia Colón Mendoza and Lisandra Estevez (Abingdon: Routledge, 2024).

4 Robert Neuman, *Baroque and Rococo Art and Architecture* (London: Pearson, 2012), 157.

the human body, with veins, humours, blood, and complexion."[5] She adds that certain wood types were favored because they could be used for detailed carvings. She notes that cedar "*de las Indias* (from the Indies)" was highly used in seventeenth-century Spain and was brought from the Americas.[6] The fact the wood was imported supports the purposeful choice of materials. As a symbol, "wood played a powerful role in aiding the sense of animation in sculpture"; authors even mention the similarities between flesh and bark.[7] Theologians associated chestnut and walnut with the Resurrection.[8] The walnut's three parts are further linked with the wood of the Trinity.[9] Sculptors understood the symbolic significance of wood and the benefits of the materials in terms of carving techniques. Often, sculptors were present to direct the tree's selection and removal.[10] Wood's lifelike characteristics, like contraction and expansion, make it ideal for creating verisimilar sculptures. Its lightweight is necessary for religious sculptures that are transported in procession. In addition, wood was used to create religious sculpture because of its role in the Bible. The material connects to the Tree of Life and the Tree of Knowledge of Good and Evil, and the former

---

5 Christina Neilson, "Carving Life: the meaning of wood in early modern European sculpture," in *The Matter of Art: Materials, Practices and Cultural Logics: c. 1250–1750*, ed. Christy Anderson, Anne Dunlop, and Pamela H. Smith (Manchester: Manchester Univ. Press, 2015), 223.

6 Neilson, "Carving Life," 224.

7 Neilson, "Carving Life," 225.

8 For Augustine see Meredith Gill, *Augustine in the Italian Renaissance: Art and Philosophy from Petrarch to Michelangelo* (Cambridge: Cambridge Univ. Press, 2005), 16–26. For Ambrose, see *Hexaemeron*, in Jacques Paul Migne, ed., *Patrologiae cursus completus: Series Latina* (Paris: Migne,1844–64), vol. 14, 179; noted by Mirel d'Ancona, *The Garden of the Renaissance: Botanical Symbolism in Italian Painting* (Firenze: Olschki, 1978), 93–95.

9 Neilson, "Carving Life," 227–28.

10 Jesús María Parrado del Olmo, *Talleres escultóricos del siglo XVI en Castilla y León: Arte como idea, arte como impresa comercial* (Valladolid: Ediciones Universidad de Valladolid, 2002), 81.

is linked to the wood used for Christ's cross.[11] Most importantly, Joseph and Christ were both carpenters and carved wood.[12]

Polychrome sculpture's materiality adds another layer of meaning to the *parangón* debate. Because no theoretical treatises existed in Spain in the sixteenth century discussing the aesthetics of polychrome sculpture, we rely on contracts and judicial documents to focus on the techniques. In architectural treatises such as Diego del Sagredo's *Las Medidas del Romano* (1526), for example, Felipe Bigarny (1475–1542) appears as a discussant defending the *tradista* (draftsman) and his technical skills and favoring Vitruvian proportions.[13] Bigarny was born in Burgundy, visited Italy, and worked in Spain. In 1513, he was named "maker and examiner of all the works of sculpture made in the Kingdom of Castille."[14] This official title marks the importance of the medium of sculpture at court and highlights his role as a sculptor. Among his collaborations, we know that a document from January 7, 1519, notes that he had a partnership with Alonso Berruguete, which included the decorations for Juan de Selvagio's burial chapel in Santa Engracia in Zaragoza.[15] José Camón Aznar further notes that Bigarny worked with Alonso Berruguete to design the Royal Chapel of Granada.[16]

---

11 The correct number of trees is a source of debate. See Tryggve Mettinger, *The Eden Narrative: A Literary and Religio-historical Study of Genesis 2–3* (Winona Lake, IN: Eisenbrauns, 2007).

12 Ilenia Colón Mendoza, *The Cristos yacentes of Gregorio Fernández: Polychrome Sculptures of the Supine Christ in Seventeenth-Century Spain* (Farnham: Ashgate, 2015), 27–32.

13 Parrado del Olmo, *Talleres escultóricos del siglo XVI en Castilla y León*, 20. See also José María de Azcárate, *Escultura del siglo XVI. Ars Hispaniae: Historia Universal del Arte Hispánico*, Vol. 13 (Madrid: Editorial Plus-Ultra, 1958), 32.

14 "Hacedor y examinador de todas las obras de talla que si hiceran en los reinos de Castilla." Parrado del Olmo, *Talleres escultóricos del siglo XVI en Castilla y León*, 29.

15 C. D. Dickerson III, "Return of to Spain, *Pintor del Rey*, and Learning to Sculpt," in *Alonso Berruguete: First Sculptor of Renaissance Spain*, ed. C. D. Dickerson III and Mark P. MacDonald (Washington, DC: National Gallery of Art, 2019), 40.

16 For an early monograph see José Camón Aznar, *Alonso Berruguete* (Madrid: Espasa-Calpe, 1980).

To further understand these theoretical discussions about polychromy, we rely on Francisco Pacheco, who states in his *Arte de la Pintura*, book 1, chapter 3, section 6: "Sculpture has existence, painting has an appearance." Therefore, polychrome sculpture is in a unique category because it has both characteristics. Pacheco contributes to the *parangón* debate already established by other art theorists, such as Pablo Cespedes' *Discurso de la Comparación de la Antiguedad y Moderna Pintura y Escultura* (1605) and Vicente Carducho's *Diálogos de la Pintura* (1633).[17] *Diálogos* is a significant precedent because, as Hellwig argues, Carducho's unique "conciliatory stance" on the *parangón* anticipates the rise of the status of sculpture.[18] Pacheco's in-depth discussion of polychrome sculpture shows his alliance with painting but, at the same time, places polychrome sculpture at a higher rank than uncolored sculpture.[19] He also mentions this in his *Arte de la Pintura*, saying: "Sculpture alone, without the life of painting, cannot deceive."[20] Pacheco gives priority to the place of painting in the production of polychrome sculpture. Pacheco is also in dialogue with sixteenth-century texts such as Lázaro de Velasco's *Los diez Libros de Arquitectura de Vitrubio*

---

17 Other sources for the Spanish *parangón* also include Juan de Jáuregui, *Diálogo entre la Naturaleza y las dos artes, Pintura y Escultura, de cuya preeminencia se disputa y juzga* (1618), Jusepe Martínez, *Discursos practicables del nobilísimo arte de la Pintura* (c.1675) and Antonio Palomino, *Museo pictórico y escala óptica* (1715–24). See Francisco Calvo Serraller, *La teoría de la pintura en el Siglo de Oro* (Madrid: Cátedra, 1981).

18 For Carducho see Karin Hellwig, "The *Paragone* between Painting and Sculpture," in *On Art and Painting: Vicente Carducho and Baroque Spain*, ed. Jean Andrews, Jeremy Roe, and Oliver Noble Wood (Cardiff: Univ. of Wales Press, 2016), 279. Hellwig explains that Carducho only references polychrome sculpture specifically in his eighth dialogue when discussing technique and touches on "statue painting" in relation to sculpture; he ignores polychrome sculpture because it does not fit with Italian "academic artistic taste," 275.

19 Pacheco opposes the use of glass eyes and prefers they be painted with a *polimento* or gloss finish. Other sculptors such as Gregorio Fernández uses *postizos* as early as 1620.

20 Francisco Pacheco, *Arte de la Pintura*, ed. F. J. Sánchez Cantón, vol. 1 (Madrid: Instituto de Valencia de Don Juan, Imprenta y Editorial Maestre, 1956), 72.

(1550–69) and *De varia commensuracion para la escultura y la arquitectura de* Juan de Arfe y Villafañe (1565) that place sculpture before painting. Notably, Juan de Arfe discusses both Felipe Bigarny and Alonso Berruguete by briefly noting the latter's use of proportions. These previously mentioned treatises establish the superiority of sculpture as it relates to the human body and architecture. Polychrome sculpture's status in the hierarchy of the arts in Spain is unique due to its use of color and also the sixteenth-century texts that promote its importance as an individual art form. At this time, Alonso Berruguete became a prominent sculptor, establishing an enduring legacy.

Berruguete in Scholarship

In the last fifteen years, exhibitions and publications on polychrome sculpture have marked a new era for studies of the medium in the English-speaking world, with exhibitions such as Xavier Bray's *The Sacred Made Real: Spanish Painting and Sculpture, 1600–1700* at the National Gallery and Ronda Kasl's *Sacred Spain: Art and Belief in the Spanish World* in Indianapolis's Museum of Art.[21] These exhibitions paved the way for a show focused solely on Alonso Berruguete's works at the National Gallery of Art in Washington, DC, in 2019. Alonso Berruguete was the son of the painter Pedro Berruguete. He was born in Paredes de Nava in 1488 and traveled to Italy in 1504. Before his return to Spain in 1518, he was appointed painter to Charles V of Spain.[22] Much scholarship has focused on his travel to Italy and the subsequent impact on his work. Two significant publications focus on the importance of his trip to Italy and his use of classicism. The first book written by Manuel Arias Martínez, *Hijo del Laocoonte: Alonso Berruguete y la antigüedad pagana*, is a catalogue that includes five essays that address topics such as the *paragone* and the importance of antiquity. The author mentions

---

21 See corresponding catalogues Xavier Bray, *The Sacred Made Real: Spanish Painting and Sculpture, 1600–1700* (London: National Gallery, 2009) and Ronda Kasl, *Sacred Spain: Art and Belief in the Spanish World* (New Haven, CT: Yale Univ. Press, 2009).

22 Dickerson, "Return of to Spain," 38.

that Berruguete oscillates between classical rules and the freedom of form. He further concludes that Berruguete's trip to Italy, his relationship with the monarchy, and his reinterpretation of antiquity are the key to his success. Berruguete's work is a synthesis of the disciplines of painting and sculpture, and in a sense, he produced "sculptural paintings."[23] A second book published in conjunction with the first solo exhibition in the United States of Berruguete's work is entitled *Alonso Berruguete: First Sculptor of Renaissance Spain*, which again focuses on the importance of his experience in Italy.[24] The title of the book can be regarded as problematic because it ignores the contributions of Felipe Bigarny, Domenico Fancelli, Diego de Siloé, and Bartolomé Ordoñez, among others, who are also labeled "Renaissance" sculptors working in Spain.[25] We know, for example, that Bigarny also traveled to Rome and benefited from his studies there. However, his work should not be valued for its lack of inherent Italianness.[26] Using stylistic elements to pinpoint when the Hispano-Flemish style switched to a truly "Renaissance" style present only in the work of Berruguete should be met with caution. Despite this, the exhibition and catalogue add to the understanding of polychrome sculpture by artists such as Berruguete and make important contributions to the research on the subject outside the scholarship published in Spain. The twelve essays included in the catalogue chronicle his career, travel to Italy, and his *retablo* production.

---

23 Manuel Arias Martínez, *Hijo del Laocoonte: Alonso Berruguete y la antigüedad pagana* (Madrid: Ministerio de Educación, Cultura y Deporte, Subdirección General de Documentación y Publicaciones: 2017), 86.
24 Dickerson and MacDonald, ed., *Alonso Berruguete*.
25 For example, the book by Manuel Gómez-Moreno, *Las Águilas del Renacimiento español: Bartolomé Ordoñéz, Diego Silóe, Pedro Machuca, Alonso Berruguete* (Madrid: Xarait, 1983) discusses this group of artists who are considered promoters of the Renaissance ideals.
26 Dickerson refers to Bigarny's style as something Berruguete would have regarded as "strangely passé" yet the market for the retablo and sculptures lies in the continued repetition of types and forms as he himself notes. There was a preference in Spain for this type of Hispano-Flemish style. See Dickerson, "Return of to Spain," 41.

Workshop Practices

Art historian Jesús María Parrado del Olmo discusses the importance and organization of Castilian workshops, noting that by 1577, the workshops in Valladolid were overcrowded. The *cartas de apprendiz* (apprentice exams) that survive reveal important information about sculpture workshop practices. Namely, Castille workshops were full of apprentices from the Basque region, Navarre, and Rioja, and some came from as far away as Portugal. This denotes their popularity and the perception that they provided a better-quality apprenticeship.[27] Surprisingly, apprentices transferred from one workshop to another. One apprentice, Pablo Villarte, began studying with Mateo Lacrin from Palencia for eight ducats for four years. Villarte then transferred to Palencia and left Valladolid. His move was perhaps because Palencia was more economical.[28] After the artists met their apprenticeship terms, they became officials. We do not have *cartas de examen* (master exams) that survive this period in Valladolid as we do in Seville. Parrado del Olmo suggests that the absence of *cartas de examen* in Castille and their lack of mention in other sources is evidence of the flexibility of the artistic practices of the region that made the test itself unnecessary.[29] Castille would have been an ideal place for Alonso Berruguete to transition from painter to sculptor after his trip to Italy.

A primary source sheds further light on the workshop practices of Berruguete's studio. There is a specific instance in 1535 where Jerónimo, the son of pharmacist Iñigo Santiago, complained that he did not receive the proper training in painting while in Berruguete's workshop.[30] This document related to the disagreement between Berruguete and Iñigo Santiago mentions a group of witnesses to the master that form part of his workshop. It is unknown if they were officials or apprentices, but they include painters and sculptors. Of all the witnesses mentioned, Gregorio Tovar, Alonso Valpuesta (painter), Francisco Giralte (sculptor), Diego de Salamanca, Pedro

---

27 Parrado del Olmo, *Talleres escultóricos del siglo XVI en Castilla y León*, 33.
28 Ibid., 35.
29 Ibid., 36.
30 Ibid., 32.

de Guaza, Pablo Ortiz (painter later in Ávila), and Iñigo Arrate, two are painters, and one is a sculptor. Parrado del Olmo concludes that Berruguete's workshops had both painters and sculptors apprenticing with him simultaneously. The size and complexity of the workshops would vary. For example, Felipe Bigarny's workshop was the most industrialized of the period. Because he had many contracts happening at the same time, he was directing concurrent projects in Burgos and Toledo and would send a group of *oficiales* (officials) and apprentices to each location.[31] When Juan de Juni (1506–77) died in 1577, the workshop of Esteban Jordán had an influx of officials and became one of the most extensive workshops in Valladolid.[32] This was possible because officials could move from one workshop to the next. The execution of multiple projects and the changes in the size of the workshops show their importance in the artistic production of the period.

The workshop master at the top of the hierarchy had no flexibility to move. There is also no evidence of exams for this rank in the workshop. Some late examples of these exams for masters survive in Andalusia from the seventeenth century for sculptors, *entalladores*, and *ensambladores*.[33] Parrado del Olmo mentions that some documents do not distinguish between official and master; the role of the master is directly correlated to the ability to finance a large workshop.[34] For example, Juan de Juni is referred to by Alonso Berruguete as an official in the *Pleito de la Antigua* (The Disagreement of la Antigua), even though we consider him a master.[35] Furthermore, Juan de Juni, a prominent artist with his own workshop, had financial problems at the end of his life, illustrating the economic complexities of the workshop system. We can conclude that Berruguete's workshop had sculptors and painters working side by side and remained, like other Castilian workshops, flexible in terms of

---

31 Ibid., 40.
32 Azcárate, *Escultura del siglo XVI. Ars Hispaniae*, 153.
33 Parrado del Olmo, *Talleres escultóricos del siglo XVI en Castilla y León*, 43.
34 Ibid., 45.
35 Ibid., 43. See also Jesús María Parrado del Olmo, *Historia del Arte de Castilla y León*. Tomo V. Renacimiento y Clasicismo. Escultura (Valladolid: Ambito Ediciones, 1996).

exams and titles. It was in this familial environment that Berruguete influenced future generations of artists.

Berruguete's Legacy

The legacy of Berruguete as an artist is evidenced in the works of his students and followers, who copy visual and stylistic elements. Inocencio Berruguete (1520–75) studied in the workshop of his uncle Alonso and likely collaborated with him in the choirstalls of the Cathedral of Toledo. In the workshop setting Alonso Berruguete taught him the art of sculpture and served as his mentor. Interestingly, Innocencio Berruguete also worked with Juan de Juni, who was also an influence on his work.[36]

The most famous of Inocencio's works is the *retablo* for the Church of Santa Eulalia in Paredes de Nava, which substituted a Gothic *retablo* by his grandfather, the painter Pedro Berruguete (1450–1503). Here, he worked with Esteban Jordán, who was Inocencio's brother-in-law.[37] The drawing (*traza*) and sculptures are by Inocencio and Jordán, and Alonso Berruguete and his school created the scene of Calvary. Inocencio Berruguete also did the grotesques at the bottom of the columns. The retablo reuses twelve wooden panels painted in oil in 1490 by Pedro Berruguete. At the center of the retablo is the Martyrdom of Saint Eulalia, patron of the church, with executioners; above is Saint Peter with his symbolic keys and Saint Paul with a sword, both by Esteban Jordán. The third tier is the *Virgin of the Assumption* by Inocencio Berruguete, the original patron of the church. Above the attic is a *Calvary of Christ* with two thieves attributed to the school of Alonso Berruguete.

---

36 For Juan de Juni, see Juan José Martín González, *Juan de Juni: Vida y Obra* (Madrid: Publicaciones del Patrimonio Nacional de Museos, 1974) and Jesús Urrea Fernández, *Juan de Juni y su época: exposición conmemorativa del IV centenario de la muerte de Juan de Juni in Valladolid*, Museo Nacional de Escultura, Apr–May 1977 and Madrid, Museo Español de Arte Contemporáneo, May–June 1977 (Madrid: Publicación del Patronato Nacional de Museos, 1977).

37 Archivo Histórico Nacional, sección Clero, Legajo 5410, Año 1559.

Esteban Jordán was born circa 1530 and died in Valladolid in 1598. He worked first in León and then in Valladolid. He was married to Felicia González Berruguete, niece of Alonso Berruguete and sister of Inocencio. His second wife, María Becerra, is believed to be related to Gaspar Becerra (1520–68).[38] Gaspar Beccera had a prolific career, worked for Philip II, and studied in Italy with Giorgio Vasari.[39] Jordán worked as the *retablo mayor* (main retable) of the Cathedral of Astorga under the supervision of Gaspar Becerra.[40] The first documented work by Jordán is the major *retablo* of the church of Santa Eulalia de Paredes de Nava in Palencia from 1556, where he worked with his brother-in-law Inocencio Berruguete, who is responsible for the *Assumption*. In 1573, Gaspar Becerra submitted the drawing for the major *retablo* of Church Santa María in Medina de Rioseco. However, it was Juan de Juni who oversaw the overall creation of the work. When Juan de Juni died, the church contracted Esteban Jordán to sculpt. He did the sculptural work, except for the figures of Saint Peter and Saint Paul, which are by Juni, and the calvary scene by Pedro de Oa, son-in-law of Jordán. The last ten years of the life of Jordán were full of activity. His fame was such that Philip II commissioned him to make the mayor retablo of the Monastery of Montserrat, drawn by Francisco de Mora, which is no longer extant.

Manuel Álvarez was born in Palencia in 1517 and died in Valladolid 1587. He is recognized for his *retablo* work. He was a student of Berruguete and related to Francisco Giralte, a follower of Berruguete, who married Manuel's sister, Isabel.[41] Álvarez and Giralte also collaborated on projects together. Álvarez established his workshop in Palencia and is known to have worked in alabaster. By the 1580s, he moved his workshop to Valladolid, which was likely taken over by his son Adrián Álvarez, a sculptor.[42] As a follower of Berruguete, his work is sometimes referred to as more traditionally classical. In the retablo of Nuestro Señora de la Asunción in Tudela de Duero, made between 1573 and 1586, he works with Juan de la

---

38 Azcárate, *Escultura del siglo XVI. Ars Hispaniae*, 285.
39 Ibid., 168.
40 Ibid., 168.
41 Ibid., 288.
42 Ibid., 291.

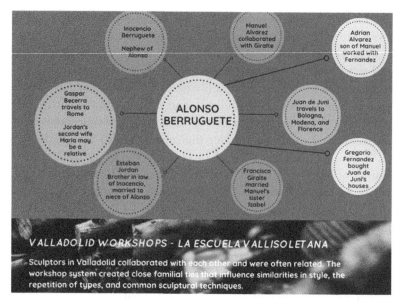

Figure 1. Valladolid Workshops Establishing Familial and Professional Ties (Diagram: Ilenia Colón Mendoza).

Maza. Here, Berruguete's direct influence is seen in the tilt of the head and position of the neck of one of the Magi.

Furthemore, Manuel's son Adrián worked with Gregorio Fernández (1576–1636) who made the *sagrario* and tabernacle located in the central of the first tier (*cuerpo*).[43] The second *cuerpo* contains a sculpture of San Miguel, also by Fernández. Álvarez carved the reliefs of the Life of Christ (Nativity, Presentation at the Temple, Resurrection, and the coming of the Holy Spirit). The coat of arms of the Condes de Fuensaldaña, patrons of the church, is at the crown of the retablo.

Berruguete's influence is extensive, and this diagram (Fig. 1) shows the connections between him and other artists, his students, their family members and collaborators, and the next generation of

---

43 For Gregorio Fernández see Mendoza, *The Cristos yacentes of Gregorio Fernández* and Juan José Martín González, *El escultor Gregorio Fernández* (Madrid: Ministerio de Cultura, 1980).

artists such as Gregorio Fernández. Sculptors in Valladolid collaborated and were often related to one another. The workshop system, where some apprentices and even officials lived with the master, created close familial ties that influenced similarities in style, the repetition of types, and standard sculptural techniques. These workshops produced many polychrome retablos, considered the cornerstone of artistic sculptural production in Spain. These *bellas composiciones* combined architecture, painting, gilding, and polychrome sculpture and show the importance of workshop collaboration. Ultimately, it is here that painters and sculptors work side by side, and Alonso Berruguete successfully made the transition from one medium to the other.

University of Central Florida

From Scripture to Spectacle: Fiction, Religion, and the Visual in Maarten van Heemskerk's *Ecce Homo* (1544)

Sunmin Cha

THIS paper explores the dynamics of fiction through an analysis of Maarten van Heemskerk's *Ecce Homo* (1544) (Fig. 1). Examining the painting in the complex context of the biblical narrative of the Passion, religious plays, and public executions, I argue that the painting encourages affective piety of devotees by engaging them in the bodily and sensory experience of looking. These findings contribute to a deeper understanding of how fictional elements in the painting intertwine with religious narratives, shaping affective piety and creating powerful connections between art, theater, and the contemporary Mass, particularly concerning the elevation of the Host. The beholder of the painting, the audience of the play, and the spectator of the juridical punishment all converge in front of Maarten van Heemskerk's *Ecce Homo*. Finally, the underlying desire to see the spectacle in each occasion is consummated with the ultimate spectacle of early modern religious life, the sacrament of the Eucharist.

The *Ecce Homo* decorated the family chapel of wealthy sheriff Jan van Drenckwaerdt in the Augustinian church in Dordrecht, the Netherlands, between about 1544 and 1572. The altarpiece, which is more than six feet wide when fully opened, features five scenes: the central panel depicts the Ecce Homo in which Pilate presents Christ to the crowd, which calls for his crucifixion; the left interior wing features the patron, Jan van Drenckwaerdt and his patron saint St. John the Evangelist; Jan's wife, Margaretha de Jonge van Baertwyck and St. Margaret of Antioch appear on the right interior wing (Fig. 1). The triptych retains its original sixteenth-century frame,

Figure 1. Maarten van Heemskerck, *Ecce Homo*, 1544, oil on panel, National Museum, Warsaw. Photo by Piotr Ligier.

which features an elaborate carved architectural surrounding for the central panel.[1]

Maarten van Heemskerck's *Ecce Homo* has received scarce scholarly attention. This is partly because most of the scholarship on Heemskerck has been devoted to his journey to Rome and its influence on the Netherlandish painters. In particular, scholars have not paid enough attention to the iconographic details in his religious paintings. Instead, they have emphasized the stylistic aspect, assigning Heemskerck's exaggerated and twisted depiction of figures as a part of Haarlem's mannerism.[2] The *Ecce Homo* occupies a much

---

1 Anne T. Woollett, Yvonne Szafran, and Alan Phenix, *Drama and Devotion: Heemskerck's Ecce Homo Altarpiece from Warsaw* (Los Angeles: The J. Paul Getty Museum, 2012), 11–17.

2 Martin van Heemskerk, Tatjana Bartsch, and Peter Seiler, eds., *Rom zeichnen: Maarten van Heemskerck 1532–1536/37*, Humboldt-Schriften zur Kunst- und Bildgeschichte, vol. 8 (Berlin: Gebr. Mann, 2012); Arthur J. DiFuria, *Maarten van Heemskerck's Rome: Antiquity, Memory, and the Cult of Ruins* (Leiden: Brill, 2019).; and Tatjana Bartsch, *Maarten van Heemskerck: Römische Studien Zwischen Sachlichkeit Und Imagination*, Römische

more important place within the painter's oeuvre than has been recognized. Many of Heemskerck's paintings were destroyed during the iconoclasm in 1566.[3] Thus, the *Ecce Homo* altarpiece provides an opportunity to reconstruct now-lost paintings by the painter and, by extension, contemporary religious thought and debates.[4]

In the following essay, I will first examine Heemskerck's *Ecce Homo* as an indexical image. The painting depicts the moment when Pilate tells people to "behold" Christ. Heemskerck's unusual depiction of the theme focuses less on the biblical narrative than on the act of seeing—beholding—itself. Then I will demonstrate that the theatricality of *Ecce Homo* evokes the viewer's experience in religious drama and public execution. The pictorial devices used by the painter, in fact, resonate with the contemporary practice of play and jurisdiction. Lastly, I will explore the painting's place and role in the spectacle of the Eucharist. The act of opening the doors of the altarpiece itself was a spectacle for the early modern viewer, culminating in the elevation of the Host. At the same time, it became the object of harsh criticism from the reform-minded group that began to take shape in the Netherlands.

The *Ecce Homo* as an Indexical Image

The central scene of this altarpiece fundamentally links the performative aspects of the narrative to the act of spectatorship. In John 19, Pilate presents Christ to the people who are asking for his execution, saying, "Behold, the man [Ecce homo]!"[5] Heem-

---

Studien Der Bibliotheca Hertziana, vol. 44 (Munich: Hirmer, 2019). Most recently, the National Museum in Warsaw conducted cleaning of the altarpiece in a collaboration with the Getty Museum. The museums published a book as a report after the cleaning, which mainly focuses on the technical aspects of the altarpiece.

3 For iconoclasm in the Netherlands and its impact on art see, Koenraad Jonckheere et al., ed., *Art after Iconoclasm: Painting in the Netherlands between 1566 and 1585* (Turnhout: Brepols, 2012).

4 David Freedberg, "Aertsen, Heemskerck En de Crisis van de Kunst in de Nederlanden," *Bulletin van Het Rijksmuseum* 35, no. 3 (1987): 224.

5 "Pilate then went out again, and said to them, 'Behold, I am bringing Him out to you, that you may know that I find no fault in Him.' Then

skerck's *Ecce Homo* emphasizes the indexical aspect of the theme in an unprecedented manner. Firstly, the frontal presentation of Christ in full view strikingly departs from the traditional representations of the narrative. As exemplified by the works of Hieronymus Bosch and Quinten Massys, the protagonists—Christ, Pilate, and his entourage—are mostly portrayed from the three-quarter view.[6] Furthermore, I argue, Heemskerck's *Ecce Homo* emphasizes the viewer's act of seeing by encouraging their identification with the jeering crowd. These soldiers and onlookers are depicted under the platform in the half-length, which is exceptional for a triptych of such a large scale. They are placed very close to the foreground and almost appear to break into the viewer's space. Due to the immediacy of the painted figures, the viewer can easily identify with them and, in turn, their act of seeing.

It is worth noting that the jeering crowd in Heemskerck's *Ecce Homo* does not show any particular hand gestures that are constantly visible in the Netherlandish paintings of the same subject. From Hieronymus Bosch to Quinten Massys, the painters paid extensive attention to the hand gestures of the onlookers. The excessive details of blasphemous gestures and careful handling of the countenance of the crowd are compelling in all these earlier examples.[7] Given that this triptych is much larger than the earlier images, the lack of hand gestures is indeed even more puzzling. Precisely because there

---

Jesus came out, wearing the crown of thorns and the purple robe. And Pilate said to them, 'Behold the Man!' Therefore, when the chief priests and officers saw Him, they cried out, saying, 'Crucify Him, crucify Him!' Pilate said to them, 'You take Him and crucify Him, for I find no fault in Him.'" John 19:4–6.

6 Larry Silver, *The Paintings of Quinten Massys with Catalogue Raisonné* (Montclair, NJ: Allanheld & Schram, 1984), 210–20. The paintings referred here are Hieronymus Bosch's *Ecce Homo* (c. 1516) in Städelsches Kunstinstitut und Städtische Galerie, Frankfurt and Quinten Massys's *Christ Presented to the People (Ecce Homo)* (c. 1515) in Museo del Prado.

7 Heemskerck's own print from the same period also includes various gestures of mocking, which suggests that the Haarlem artist was well aware of the pictorial convention. See, Dirck Volkertsz Coornhert after Maarten van Heemskerck, *Ecce Homo*, 1544, from the series *The Fall and Salvation of Mankind through the Life and Passion of Christ*, 1548. Etching, 24.5 x 19.2 cm. British Museum, London.

is no detailed depiction of blasphemous gestures, the crowd's reaction is solely conveyed by their act of seeing. Finally, at the very center of the triptych, a man torturing Christ immediately captures the viewer's attention. Standing slightly behind the two most important protagonists of the narrative, Christ and Pilate, he makes powerful eye contact with the viewer.

Theatricality in the *Ecce Homo*

Such emphasis on the spectatorship of the viewer is, in fact, closely related to the contemporary playgoer's experience.[8] In the *Ecce Homo*, the distinction between the painting and reality is constantly challenged. Indeed, one of the distinctive features of medieval religious drama is the lack of designated and fixed boundaries. In contrast to the modern theater and play-going experience, medieval plays and performances took place outdoors, for example, in a central marketplace and the streets. A handful of surviving stage illustrations offer valuable insight into the physical form of the early modern stage and its theatrical productions. Hubert Cailleau's drawing of 1547, for instance, provides a picture of the key sites included in contemporary Passion plays. It is a frontispiece for a manuscript containing a cycle of plays performed in Valenciennes. The description says: "the theatre or stage as it was when the Passion of our Lord was performed in 1547."[9] The drawing shows the different stages that would be used for the entire performance.

---

8 M. C. Bradbrook, "An 'Ecce Homo' of the Sixteenth Century and the Pageants and Street Theatres of the Low Countries," *Shakespeare Quarterly* 9, no. 3 (1958): 426; and Martin Stevens, "The Intertextuality of Late Medieval Art and Drama," *New Literary History* 22, no. 2 (1991): 328.

9 Laura Weigert, "'Theatricality' in Tapestries and Mystery Plays and Its Afterlife in Painting," in *Theatricality in Early Modern Art and Architecture*, ed. Caroline van Eck and Stijn Bussels (Hoboken, NJ: John Wiley & Sons, 2011), 24. Hubert Cailleau, "Stage" for the 1547 Passion play in Valencienne, detail, ("Le Mystère par personages de la vie, passion, mort, resurrection et ascension de Notre Seigneur Jésus-Christ en 25 journées"), 1577. Paris, Bibliothèque Nationale de France, MS Fr. Rothschild 3010 (I.7.3), frontispiece.

Between the poles of Heaven and Hell at opposite ends of the stage, several three-walled "mansions" appear. These mansions would be scattered around the city spaces. The plan for the Lucerne Passion Play (*Osterspiel*) of 1583 remains today. It shows how the stage and various set items were arranged on the wine market square in Lucerne. Scaffolds surrounded the square all around, representing various places as the passion story unfolded.[10]

In addition, the transitional zones between the scaffolds were also important spaces for plays. This "zone of transition" was never firmly defined but rather was a malleable place where movement between two defined locations or times was enacted. The nondescript zone between stages was also where the audience would view the play, with actors moving among them from scaffold to scaffold. It was the space where the distinction between the audience and actors became blurred. A sixteenth-century painting of the *Ecce Homo* (1554–98) by Gillis Mostaert (1528—98) shows this characteristic of the early modern stage. In his painting, Pilate presents Christ from the elevated porch of the old *Stadhuis* (city hall) in Antwerp.[11] The painter transformed Antwerp into the Holy Land. City hall became Pilate's hall, and its citizenry became a jeering crowd. Of more importance, in the right foreground, Barabbas is

---

10 Mark Todd Trowbridge, "Art and Ommegangen: Paintings, Processions, and Dramas in the Late-Medieval Low Countries" (PhD diss., New York University, 2000), 33–34.

11 The painting is also called *Passion Play on the City Square in Antwerp*. It is reasonable to assume that the painting faithfully reflects the condition of the buildings around the mid-sixteenth century. The actual town hall, a rather modest Gothic building with typical corner towers and stepped gable was erected at the beginning of the fifteenth century on the site of the older bread house, which had already been occupied by the municipal services. The building is accurately depicted down to its parts. One notices the facade with a double staircase leading to the main entrance, under the curly arch above the entrance, a sculpture group with Our Lady, the patron saint of the city, partially unfinished statues for royal portraits, and at the very top, the coat of arms of the duke of Burgundy with two angels as shield holders. Jean F. Buck, "GILLIS MOSTAERT - CHRISTUS DOOR PILATUS AAN HET VOLK GETOOND," Openbaar Kunstbezit Vlaanderen, accessed May 24, 2024, https://www.okv.be/artikel/gillis-mostaert-christus-door-pilatus-aan-het-volk-getoond.

led away directly by the onlookers. Therefore, multi-staged dramas transformed the city into a theater, whether processional or fixed. Audiences were actively involved in the performances, where there was no firm divide between themselves and the stage.[12] Lines directly address the audience and emphasize the audience's active involvement, especially with their act of seeing. For instance, in a fifteenth-century French passion play, we read, "Open your eyes and look / you devout people who are waiting to hear something salvific."[13] Such addresses to the audience are found in almost all religious plays.[14] The most compelling example is Christ's direct address to the audience. In York Corpus Christi Plays, Christ speaks from the cross: "Every man who walks by way or street, pay attention that you miss none of this affliction. Behold my head, my hands, and my feet, and truly understand anew as you pass by."[15]

In particular, the narrative of the Ecce Homo is significant in two ways: spiritually, it is the salvific sacrifice of Christ. It was the moment when the humanity of Christ was emphasized, and the unbelieving people denied his divinity. Theatrically, it is the very self-conscious creation of spectacle, as showing and presenting the bare life of Christ. In York Corpus Christi Plays, the sight of Christ, especially his bodily presence, is the central theme when Christ encounters Pilate. When Christ enters the scene, Pilate speaks of an involuntary reverential response:

Such a *sight* was never yet seen.
Come sit,
My control was taken from me completely—

---

12 Trowbridge, "Art and Ommegangen," 35.

13 "Ouvrez vos yeulx et regardez / devotes gens qui actendez a oyr chose salutaire." Translation from Gabriella Mazzon, *Pathos in Late-Medieval Religious Drama and Art: A Communicative Strategy* (Leiden and Boston, MA: Brill Rodopi, 2018), 241.

14 Erika Fischer-Lichte, "The medieval religious plays—ritual or theater?," in *Visualizing Medieval Performance: Perspectives, Histories, Contexts*, ed. Elina Gertsman (Aldershot and Burlington, VT: Ashgate, 2008.), 249.

15 Jill Stevenson, *Performance, Cognitive Theory, and Devotional Culture: Sensual Piety in Late Medieval York* (New York: Palgrave Macmillan, 2010), 147.

I stood up, I could not restrain myself
From honoring him in deed and in thought. (33. 271–75)[16]

Arousing a bodily response from Pilate, Christ's body and presence itself became a powerful spectacle. Heemskerck was also closely associated with the visual languages of drama and plays. It has been suggested that the painter was a member of a chamber of rhetoric and designed a device for a Haarlem chamber. A contemporary illustration of the stage used in Antwerp on the occasion of a festival in 1561 shows a striking resemblance to the edifices depicted on the chamber of rhetoric device designed by Heemskerck. Indeed, the members of the Haarlem chamber staged the Play of Ecce Homo in 1534 and another Ecce Homo in 1548.[17] However, Heemkserck's *Ecce Homo* must not be taken literally as the record of an actual performance or the pictorial representation of drama. Instead, I follow a scholarly approach, which sees painting and performance as interactive texts. To see a play in the streets of early modern cities, the audience had to carry a perspective that was not unlike that provided for the viewers of Heemsckerck's painting.[18]

The Spectacle of Public Execution

The intensive emphasis on the act of seeing in the *Ecce Homo* may have been referring to the contemporary practice of public executions as well. Admittedly, public executions were spectacles in early modern European societies. Huizinga famously described the popularity of public executions:

---

16 Original: "Silke a sight was neuere ʒit sene. / Come sytt, / My comfort was caught fro me clene— / I vpstritt, I me might noʒt abstene / To wirschip hym in wark and in witte."Translation from ibid., 122.

17 Ilja M. Veldman, *Maarten van Heemskerck and Dutch Humanism in the Sixteenth Century* (Maarssen: G. Schwartz, 1977), 123–26.

18 Charlotte Steenbrugge, *Drama and Sermon in Late Medieval England: Performance, Authority, Devotion* (Kalamazoo: Medieval Institute Publications, Western Michigan University, 2017), 96–97; and Claire Sponsler, *Drama and Resistance: Bodies, Goods, and Theatricality in Late Medieval England* (Minneapolis: Univ. of Minnesota Press), 1997, 150.

... most frequent of all, one might almost say, uninterrupted, [were] the executions. The cruel excitement and coarse compassion raised by an execution formed an important item in the spiritual food of the common people. They were spectacular plays with a moral.[19]

The pillory and the scaffold where the executions take place are always erected in the most frequented place of the city, on the main square, near the hall or the market, where often religious plays were staged.

The concept of public execution as a spectacle is dramatically captured in Jean Fouquet's miniature of *The Martyrdom of St. Apollonia*. The theatrical setting fills the back of the image, enclosing and framing the action. The martyrdom of the saint is staged on the elevated platform. At the center, the saint is lying on her inclined *chevalet* while the henchmen inflict various tortures on her body. It compellingly shows the spectacular nature of violence and execution.[20] One pulls her long blond hair, two tug at the ropes that tie her, and a last one extracts her teeth with ridiculously long pincers. The unusual setting gives further insight that, as he imagines a scene and transcribes it on the page or the panel. Fouquet, in effect, stages it for the viewer. Because he depicted only half of the round theater in the background and left the scene open, we are invited to watch the spectacle of martyrdom.[21]

Moreover, as already pointed out by numerous scholars, the late medieval images of the Ecce Homo borrow their motives from medieval executions in real life. For instance, Martin Stevens suggested that the Ecce Homo scene in Hans Memling's *Passion of Christ* is completely "medievalized" and brought into Memling's own time frame.[22] Artists even borrowed a specific motif from the

---

19 Johan Huizinga, *The Waning of the Middle Ages* (Mineola, NY: Dover, 1999), 3.
20 Leslie Abend Callahan, "The Torture of Saint Apollonia: Deconstructing Fouquet's Martyrdom Stage," *Studies in Iconography* 16 (1994): 126.
21 Véronique Plesch, "Word and Image in Early Performance," in *The Routledge Research Companion to Early Drama and performance* ed. Pamela M. King (Abingdon: Routledge, 2016), 110–11.
22 Stevens, "The Intertextuality," 332–33.

contemporary practice of criminal trials. The Braunschweig Master's *Ecce Homo with the Two Thieves and Barabbas* shows Pilate presenting the captive Christ to a mob of jeering and curing Jews. In this painting, the presence of crowds, the scenography of the town hall, and its adjoining urban spaces effectively visualize the spectacular aspect of the moment of sentencing. Beneath the parapet, the two thieves and Barabbas are shown displayed in irons. The depiction of irons is realistic but rare in the images of the Ecce Homo. In turn, such detail intensifies the punitive vocabulary of the image rather than biblical and narrative accuracy.[23]

In this respect, we can turn our attention to an unusual detail in Heemskerck's *Ecce Homo*. Christ reveals his bare chest without the covering of a purple robe. As Erwin Panofsky observed, the motif of a purple robe is invariably consistent in the Ecce Homo images.[24] By contrast, Heemskerck's other Ecce Homo triptych, currently in Frans Hals Museum, also introduced an interesting motif, the hangman's rope. It is so conspicuously displayed on the bare chest of Christ. Early modern viewers might more readily understand such anachronistic and non-biblical detail as a reference to contemporary corporal punishment.[25] The motif of rope is even more significant in our context, as it was adopted as a fictional element in religious plays. The *Donaueschingen* passion play depicts at length how the Jewish executioners forcibly pulled Christ's body apart with ropes so that his body would fit into the holes on the Cross. There is no such story in the Bible. Instead, it was an allusion to the fifteenth-century torture of stretching, in which the criminal was pulled apart with ropes during interrogation.[26] Likewise, the rope on Christ's chest would have evoked the viewer's viewing experience of execution, even in a theater. Once again, the distinction between the painted

---

23 Mitchell B. Merback, *The Thief, the Cross, and the Wheel: Pain and the Spectacle of Punishment in Medieval and Renaissance Europe* (Chicago: Univ. of Chicago Press, 1999), 132–33.

24 Erwin Panofsky, "Jean Hey's 'Ecce Homo,' Speculations about Its Author, Its Donor, and Its Iconography," *Bulletin des Musées Royaux des Beaux-Arts* 6 (1956): 108–13.

25 Valentin Groebner, *Defaced: The Visual Culture of Violence in the Late Middle Ages* (New York: Zone Books, 2004), 100.

26 Ibid., 100–101.

image, the theatrical representation, and the juridical spectacle, in reality, becomes obscure.

The Spectacle of the Sacrament of the Eucharist

Above all, an altarpiece was a spectacle itself. As it appears at the central panel of a winged triptych, laypeople can only see the *Ecce Homo* for the limited occasions when the triptych was to be opened. Most of the time, the viewer would have encountered the closed state of the altarpiece, which shows St. John the Evangelist and St. Margaret of Antioch painted in grisaille on the left and right exterior panels (Figs. 2 and 3).[27] In church contexts, the opening and closing of the triptych were closely linked to the celebration of the Mass.[28] The testament of Marthe Oliviers in 1582 specified the requirements for the chapel: "Likewise, [she] desired to be placed above her and her husband's tomb her painting of our beloved Lady, standing on the sun, [with] Saint John the Baptist and Saint John the Evangelist on the doors, with a metal candlestick standing in front of it, whereupon [on] all four feast days one shall place a wax candle of one-half pound and [shall] light the same candle during the High Mass [on] all Sundays and feast days; for the candle to be lit and [for] the painting to be open and shut ... the sexton of the church every year will receive six pennies."[29] The clear implication here is that the painting was open and shut in conjunction with the lighting of the candle, which, in turn, was done in conjunction with the celebration of the Mass. Thus, within a church, some triptychs, whether functioning as altarpieces or epitaphs, were opened in relation to the liturgical ceremony.

In this respect, the choice of the subject, the *Ecce Homo*, as the central panel is significant. In the late medieval usage, the phrase Ecce Homo had acquired a significance beyond the narrative

---

27 The visual and theatrical effect of opening and closing of the altarpiece is exceptionally captured in the video recording made by the Getty Museum: https://youtu.be/pu9VTPfg1HQ?si=MHlXkYj8PyYzRYoG.

28 Lynn F. Jacobs, *Opening Doors: The Early Netherlandish Triptych Reinterpreted* (University Park, PA: Penn State Univ. Press, 2012), 8.

29 Ibid., 8–10.

Figure 2. Maarten van Heemskerck, *St. John the Evangelist* (closed state of fig.1., left exterior wing), 1544, oil on panel, 183.5 x 62.5 cm, National Museum, Warsaw, Photo by Piotr Ligier.

Figure 3. Maarten van Heemskerck, *St. Margaret of Antioch* (closed state of fig.1., right exterior wing), 1544, oil on panel, 183.5 x 62.5 cm, National Museum, Warsaw. Photo by Piotr Ligier.

elaboration from the mouth of Pilate. The words "Behold the Man" were taken to be addressed to the community of the faithful rather than to the hostile Jews. The phrase had come to designate the human nature of Christ wherever it is presented to devotees as a meditational material or as the guise of the host at Mass. Ludolph of Saxony (c. 1295—1378) said, for instance: "the sacrament of the altar commemorates the Passion of the Lord, and Christ has suffered according to His human nature; for according to his divine nature he is incapable of suffering, wherefore the priest, when elevating the host, might more fittingly say 'behold the man' than 'behold God.'"[30] The images of the Ecce Homo, thus, are no longer Christ presented to the mocking crowd, but rather Christ presented to the viewer.

The sacrament of the Eucharist is the moment of spectacle. To "see" the Host was the most important element for late medieval devotees. The fifteenth-century Augustinian monk attested to such enthusiasm as "they come when they hear bell, entering to see elevation, and when it is over they leave running and fleeing, as if they have seen the devil." Sometimes, the laypersons even shouted back to the priest and asked him to raise the host higher.[31] The act of seeing the Elevation had far more significance beyond our expectation as the image, rather than the eye, was considered to be the active agent of sight. Before the seventeenth century, the image was believed to penetrate the passive eye to make a mental impression on the viewer. Thus, when viewers see the consecrated Host, they participate in an act of communion because the real presence of Christ has entered their bodies.[32] The German phrase *Augenkommunion* (which translates to ocular communion) demonstrates the importance of seeing in the liturgy. In sum, Maarten van Heemskerck's *Ecce Homo* encourages the viewer to physically and bodily behold the Host elevated by the priest. Heemskerck's theatrical

---

30 Panofsky, "Jean Hey's 'Ecce Homo,'" 110–11.

31 Caroline Walker Bynum, *Holy Feast and Holy Fast: The Religious Significance of Food to Medieval Women* (Berkeley: Univ. of California Press, 1987), 55.

32 Henry Martin Luttikhuizen, "Late Medieval Piety and Geertgen Tot Sint Jan's 'Altarpiece for the Haarlem Jansheren'" (PhD diss., University of Virginia, 1997), 200.

and punitive reference would provoke the embodied experience of viewing religious plays and public executions. In turn, it intensifies the viewer's act of seeing in the sacrament, which Robert Scribner termed the "sacramental gaze," distinguishing it from a mystical or meditational gaze.[33]

Epilogue

Maarten van Heemskerck's *Ecce Homo* directly engages with the viewer's act of seeing by depicting the extensive acts of seeing biblical figures. This emphasis on corporeal sight is somewhat puzzling, given that it was made when using images in religious devotion was questioned and criticized. In 1533, on June 12, Corpus Christi was celebrated in Amsterdam as it was Corpus Christi Day, the feast day of the Holy Sacrament. During the procession, a group of townsmen, sheltered in a small wooden office building, ostentatiously closed the shutters of the windows that looked down onto the passing route as a sign of their disrespect. They then brazenly interrupted the sacred procession, insulting the priest and the marchers by yelling: "Rain better! Rain better! So may the priest and his God get wet!"[34]

This incident illustrates how late medieval Christian images and materiality increasingly came under pressure during the Age of Reformation. As Freedberg accurately pointed out, the iconoclastic debate in the sixteenth-century Netherlands should not be regarded as mere "background" of the painter's career during this time. The criticism of paintings was not only the theological and political debate, but it threatened the raison d'être of painters.[35] In

---

33 Robert W. Scribner, *Religion and Culture in Germany (1400–1800)* (Boston, MA: Brill, 2001), 90.

34 Henk Van Nierop, "Sacred Space Contested: Amsterdam in the Age of the Reformation," in *The Power of Space in Late Medieval and Early Modern Europe: The Cities of Italy, Northern France and the Low Countries*, ed. Marc Boone Martha Howell, Studies in European Urban History (1100–1800), vol. 30 (Turnhout: Brepols, 2013), 153–61.

35 Freedberg, "Aertsen, Heemskerck En de Crisis van de Kunst," 232–36.

fact, the series of prints made in the later period of Heemskerck's career show that the painter was well aware of contemporary image debates.[36]

In this context, the outward gaze in the *Ecce Homo* (Fig. 1) might be read as a warning or even a condemnatory message to the viewer. As Alberti described in the fifteenth century, the figures looking out "with ferocious expression and forbidding glance challenges them [the viewers] not to come near, as if he wished their business to be secret, or points to some danger or some remarkable secret."[37] Could it be, then, the torturer behind Christ and Pilate in the *Ecce Homo* warns the viewer of the painting? What the painting or painter tried to convey to contemporary viewers remains uncertain. Furthermore, regardless of the painter's intention, the viewer could have seen the *Ecce Homo* differently according to their own experience. What is clear, however, is that Maarten van Heemskerck's *Ecce Homo* addresses the "act of seeing" of the viewer, which provides a rich context of viewing experience and image debates that goes well beyond the narrative representation of the biblical story.

Columbia University

---

36 Jeremy D. Bangs, "Maerten van Heemskerck's Bel and the Dragon and Iconoclasm," *Renaissance Quarterly* 30, no. 1 (1977): 8–11; and Eleanor A. Saunders, "A Commentary on Iconoclasm in Several Print Series by Maarten van Heemskerch," *Simiolus: Netherlands Quarterly for the History of Art* 10, no. 2 (1978): 59–83. The often-cited engraving of van Heemskerck is *Destruction of the Temple of Ashtoreth, Chemosh and Milcom* (1569).

37 Leon Battista Alberti, *On Painting*, trans. Cecil Grayson (New York: Penguin, 1991), 77–78.

In the Wake of the Emperor: The Depiction of Don Carlos of Austria as *Miles Christi* in Juan de Angulo's Illustrated Manuscript[1]

Gerardo Rappazzo Amura

Don Carlos of Austria, son of Philip II and Princess Mary of Portugal, was born in 1545. He faced physical disabilities and had a controversial personality, making his claim to the Spanish throne challenging. His health deteriorated in 1557, and his behavioral disorders worsened after a severe accident in 1562. While staying at the University of Alcalá de Henares, the young prince suffered a head injury and came close to losing his life when he fell down some stairs while pursuing a young lady.[2]

---

1 This research has been conducted while benefiting from a Grant under the *Programa de Formación de Profesorado Universitario* of the Spanish Ministry of Universities (reference: FPU21/01188), within the framework of the established research group *Arte y pensamiento* (UNED - ISSN: 2530-7150). I express my gratitude to Dr. Antonio Urquízar Herrera for the suggestions he provided after reviewing the original paper. Unless noted otherwise, English translations of Latin and Spanish texts are my own.

2 Juan de Angulo, *Relación de la christiana rogativa que con cristianísimo corazón la imperial ciudad de Toledo hizo por la salud del muy alto y muy poderoso Príncipe don Carlos nuestro señor príncipe de España, cuando supo el improviso y súbito desastre que le aconteció a su alteza estando en la villa de Alcalá de Henares año de MDLXII*, manuscript, Real Biblioteca del Monasterio de San Lorenzo del Escorial, b-IV-18, fol. 34r, n.d. [hereafter cited as *Relación de la christiana rogativa*]; Luis Cabrera de Córdoba, *Historia de Felipe II, rey de España*, 1619 (Madrid: Aribau, 1876), 348–49; Jerónimo

In short, political difficulties, strained relations with his father, and imprisonment followed. Carlos died in July 1568 under unclear circumstances, and his troubled relationship with Philip II inspired local and world-famous artistic works including Verdi's remarkable opera (*Don Carlo*, 1867).[3] The drawn portrait that we will examine in this paper is part of the manuscript that narrates the events that unfolded in Toledo because of the aforementioned princely incident. The significance of this primary source lies in its meticulous portrayal of social practices—in our specific context, public ceremonies, and festivities—"whose primary purpose was to serve as political propaganda for the Iberian monarchy and the Catholic religion, intended to transform the population into active participants in a particular ideology."[4]

This article will analyze a sketch of Don Carlos's military equestrian portrait, which belongs to the *Relación de la christiana rogativa* and was composed between 1562 and 1565.[5] The author will demonstrate how this image and its literary discourse illustrate the intersection of art, history, and social practices, reflecting the political and social context of its production, with the greater goal of exploring the intentions behind its creation. To do so, I will elucidate both its symbolic meaning and the political context in which

---

de Quintana, *A la muy antigua, noble y coronada villa de Madrid. Historia de su antigüedad, nobleza y grandeza* (Madrid: Imprenta del Reyno,1629), fol. 338v.

3 Among the main writers who have addressed the topic, we can mention: Diego Jiménez de Enciso, Juan Pérez de Montalbán, Pierre de Bourdeille, César Vichard, Thomas Otway, Jean-Galbert de Campistron, Vittorio Alfieri, Louis Sebastien Mercier, Friedrich Schiller, and Friedrich de la Motte Fouqué.

4 Angela Sanz Baso, "Santos y herejes, la lucha contra el infiel en las festividades religiosas del Reino de Toledo entre 1565 y 1622," *Eikón Imago*, 15 (2020): 209–26.

5 We will use the pagination of the digital version of the document to avoid any confusion with the pencil, ink, and crossed-out numbering in the original. In the context of Early Modern history in Spain, a *relación* is a written report that provides a detailed account of a historical, political, or social event, including descriptions of the people and places involved. The document offers a complete depiction of the rogation days held in Toledo from May 6 to May 22, 1562.

it was used to legitimize the exercise of power within the Spanish Habsburg dynasty.

The Culture of Gift-giving at the Court of Philip II

The 3rd Marquis of Falces, Don Gastón de Peralta y Bosquet, presented a magnificent gift to Philip II's heir: the manuscript containing the account of rogations held in Toledo for the prince's recovery; its author was the not widely recognized writer Juan Ruiz de Angulo.[6] Displaying liberality, Prince Don Carlos rewarded the writer with 550 *reales* for the dedicated book.[7] In the same narrative, the nobleman aimed to showcase his worth, through the defense that the author of the manuscript makes of him, emphasizing his efficient performance as the *corregidor*[8] of Imperial City and underscoring the need for upright officials "of remarkable talent" to govern the Spanish "expanded empire."[9]

The portrait we will focus on is part of this gift, representing the sixteenth-century culture of gift-giving and patronage networks in courtly settings. It highlights the significance of gift-giving as a social practice, embodying concepts such as liberality and magnanimity associated with the ideal prince. Both princes and courtiers engaged in gift-giving to further their interests. The effects of royal generosity are decisive, as the prince becomes "the owner of his subjects." This dialectical relationship also implies that the vassal influences the lord. Hamish Scott summarizes this practice as follows:

---

6   The writer's name is mentioned in the manuscript: Angulo, *Relación de la christiana rogativa*, fols. 1v, 2r, 9r, 74v. He is identified as "a resident of Toledo and a native of the Angulo Valley" (Sagrario López Poza, "Emblemas españoles manuscritos en Toledo en 1562," in *Literatura emblemática hispánica: actas del I Simposio Internacional 1996*, ed. Sagrario López Poza (A Coruña: Universidade da Coruña, 1996), 135.

7   *Asiento de pago a Juan de Angulo*, March 1567, Archivo General de Simancas, Contaduría Mayor de Cuentas, 1ª época, legajo 1110.

8   Don Gastón de Peralta was appointed as the *corregidor* of the city of Toledo by King Philip II in 1559. The *corregidor* was a local administrative and judicial officer responsible for governing and maintaining order in a town or region.

9   Angulo, *Relación de la christiana rogativa*, fols. 75r–v.

"The court now is seen as the principal site where the compact between crown and nobility, which strengthened both, was negotiated and sealed."[10] Considering this, the examination of gift-giving culture, along with associated customs and rituals, sheds light on the competition for power and the conversion of wealth into political capital, as discussed by Pierre Bourdieu.[11] The political context around the production of this present was complex: while Don Carlos aspired to legitimize his position in the Council of State, the Grandees of Spain aimed to obtain appointments such as those of the prince's tutor, Gentleman of the Household, Lord High Steward, or Viceroy of the American territories, to name just a few of the most coveted positions. It seems clear that

> [the] possession of a court office increased the status of a noble family, who competed avidly to secure theses posts, believing that it would enhance their status and provide opportunities for advancements. [...] At many courts leading families established near hereditary control over the major offices and so dominated the distribution of patronage.[12]

In this context of courtly competition, gifts such as that of Gastón de Peralta were not the exception but rather the rule.[13] Hence, the portrayal of the formidable soldier of Christ was formulated within a context of shared political objectives, including the validation of the value of a vulnerable heir, who will ultimately hold power in the future and wield the ability to grant patronage.

---

10 Hamish Scott, "Aristocrats and nobles," in *Early Modern Court Culture*, ed. Erin Griffey (New York: Routledge, 2022), 98.

11 Pierre Bourdieu, "Los tres estados del capital cultural," *Sociológica* 5 (1979): 11–17; Pierre Bourdieu and Loïc Wacquant, *Una invitación a la sociología reflexiva* (Buenos Aires: Siglo XXI Editores, 1992), 178.

12 Scott, "Aristocrats and nobles," 102–3.

13 Francisco Puerto Sarmiento, *El príncipe don Carlos de Austria. Un hombre desesperado. Historia y leyenda* (Madrid: Sanz y Torres, 2022), 255–60; Jemma Field, "Female dress," in *Early Modern Court Culture*, ed. Erin Griffey (New York: Routledge, 2022), 400.

Contextualizing the Production: Threats Looming over the Spanish Empire

Referencing a war implies understanding the set of circumstances in which an armed conflict unfolds. It is evident that this is not the focus of this article, although we must recall some of the war episodes that influenced cultural production during the mid-sixteenth century. The life trajectory of Don Carlos ran parallel to some of the most notable political events in Early Modern Europe, such as the celebration of the Ecumenical Council of Trent (1545–63) and significant military episodes like the Schmalkaldic War, including the crucial Battle of Mühlberg (1547) in the Holy Roman Empire, or the Great Siege of Malta (1565). The Spanish crown's heir lived amidst the theological-political upheaval caused by the Reformation, the fratricidal struggle among Christians,—Catholics against French Huguenots, German Lutherans, and Flemish Calvinists— or the Turkish threat in the Mediterranean.

Wars against the Turks were certainly an additional complication to the issues mentioned above. The Ottoman expansion, led by Suleiman the Magnificent (1494–1566), generated fear and concern among European rulers, who saw it as a danger to their territories, power, and the supremacy of Christianity.[14]

Artistic creation, as a cultural product, was mediated by the briefly described war context. The image of the *miles Christi* cannot be understood apart from the complex and multifaceted socio-political situation of the years 1562 to 1566 or the preceding decades.

---

14 In this regard, the correspondence of the ambassador in Genoa, Gómez Suárez de Figueroa, to Emperor Charles V, King Philip II, or Regent Juana de Austria, Princess of Portugal, and Governor of the Kingdoms of Spain, or that of Andrea Doria, Prince of Melfi, to the same recipients, is enlightening.

Building an Iconography of the Counter-Reformation: The Destruction of the Other-infidel

The reader of the *Relación de la christiana rogativa* encounters a "novelized description" of events if we allow for the anachronism of such characterization. This description appears to align more closely with the author's ideological premises than with the historical circumstances that transpired. The images serve as "documentary" support for invented stories that seek to present themselves as real, imparting a clear propagandistic function to the narration. This takes place alongside the text of the relation itself, which seems to confine its focus to the chronicle of events. The author provides a comprehensive sensory experience of the *rogativas*, with the images contributing visual reinforcement within their own discursive framework. This manuscript is extraordinary due to the inclusion of anonymous hand-drawn illustrations that complement the written account, providing guidance on how these images should be interpreted by the public. The artist used sepia ink for the sketches, intended for use in xylography. Thirteen stories skillfully combine images and words where the anonymous author created several overlapping "masks" to portray the heir. Among all of them, the *miles Christi* stands out.[15]

The triumphal image of the surviving prince reaches its climax with the equestrian portrait of the soldier of Christ (fol. 78v). In addition to the illustration, the author presents us with texts—in Romance and Latin languages—organized into three epigrams, two sonnets, and a gloss in two columns (see Fig. 1).

The personification of "Faith," holding a scale model of a cathedral, reveals to us the ultimate meaning of the celebration: after the immense joy of Carlos' healing, he is now called to defend the true religion and destroy its enemies:

Atiende pues as ganado
gloriosa vida en el suelo,

---

[15] In addition to the mask of the victorious hero *all'antica*, the one of the praying prince is of utmost interest. For further information, see Gerardo Rappazzo Amura, "Don Carlos de Austria (1545–1568), *exemplum* de príncipe orante en un manuscrito ilustrado de Juan de Angulo," *Hipogrifo*, 11, no. 2 (2023): 721–51.

Figure 1. Juan de Angulo, *Relación de la christiana rogativa de Toledo por la salud del Príncipe Carlos*, fol. 78v, n.d., anonymous cartoonist, paper, pen and sepia ink, 203 x 135 mm. Photograph: Real Biblioteca del Monasterio de El Escorial, Patrimonio Nacional, b-IV-18. Reproduction rights granted by Patrimonio Nacional, available by CC-BY license.

que ganes la que es del cielo
en defensa de mi estado.[16]

[So, pay attention, for you have earned
a glorious life on Earth,
may you also win the one from Heaven,
defending my estate.]

But who are the enemies of the Faith that the prince must protect it from? Angulo makes it clear: they are the "*perfida Luteri gens*," the perfidious people of Luther. Following in the footsteps of the Christian Visigothic kings and his grandfather, Emperor Charles V, Don Carlos is called to be the new menace to the Other[17]. Despite all the laudatory symbolism associated with the soldier of the Lord, it is important to note that the Spanish heir never actually fought in defense of religion. The image provides a desirable representation of the prince that does not correspond to historical reality.

Visual Background

We are unsure about the exact graphic sources the artist used to create this image, but we can mention some works that, due to their formal and contextual similarities, may have influenced the process of creating this emblem. The visual precursors can be classified into two groups: a) the equestrian figure of the prince; and b) the enemies at the horse's feet.

---

16 Angulo, *Relación de la Christiana rogativa*, fol. 78v.

17 The concept of the "Other" refers to the perception of individuals or groups as different or foreign from the societal norm, reinforcing social boundaries and hierarchies. The process of Othering can lead to stereotyping, discrimination, and the marginalization of those deemed different. For us, the concept is crucial in understanding social identity, power dynamics, and the construction of social hierarchies within Early Modern society.

The Equestrian Figure of the Prince

As the earliest antecedents, we could point to the engraving of *Maximilian I on horseback* by Hans Burgkmair (dated 1508, printed 1518)[18] which is a clear predecessor to all later Habsburg equestrian portraits.[19] The anonymous panel painting of *Charles V in Armor and Holding a Sword* (ca. 1515) remains significant only as a testament to a tradition within the lineage, as Miguel Falomir explains.[20] Much closer in time, the artist might have drawn indirect inspiration from Titian's *Charles V at the Battle of Mühlberg* (1548), a work with immense political connotations as it presents a clear image of the *miles Christianus* in the context of the struggle against German Protestant princes. This is not the place to discuss whether the interpretations, primarily political and secondarily religious, by E. Panofsky, F. Checa, D. Bodart, M. Mancini, A. Soler del Campo or M. Falomir are appropriate, but we would like to point out that, in our opinion, they should be nuanced.[21]

---

18 Hans Burgkmair, *Emperor Maximilian I on Horseback*, 1518, woodcut, seventh state of seven (Hollstein), 32.3 × 22.7 cm., 20.64.24, The Metropolitan Museum of Art.

19 Fernando Checa Cremades, *Carlos V, a caballo, en Mühlberg de Tiziano* (Madrid: TF Editores, 2001), 52; Fernando Checa Cremades, "Caballos y caballeros: sobre la iconografía ecuestre de la Casa de Austria en España," in *Nobleza y retrato ecuestre en el arte*, ed. Ramón Maria Serrera (Seville: Real Maestranza de Caballería de Sevilla, 2015), 201–17.

20 Anonymous South German painter, *Charles V in Armor and Holding a Sword*, ca. 1515, oil on pine panel, 59.7 × 42.2 cm., SL.5.2019.34.2, The Metropolitan Museum of Art (temporary loan from Kunsthistorisches Museum, Vienna, Gemäldegalerie).

21 Erwin Panofsky, *Tiziano. Problemas de iconografía* (Madrid: Akal, 2003); Fernando Checa Cremades, *Carlos V, a caballo*; Diane Bodart, *Pouvoirs du portrait sous les Habsbourg d'Espagne* (Paris: CTHS–INHA, 2011); Matteo Mancini, "El emperador Carlos V a caballo en Mühlberg de Tiziano, un icono para la Historia del Arte," in *La restauración de El emperador Carlos V en Mühlberg a caballo de Tiziano* (Madrid: Museo Nacional del Prado, 2001), 103–16; Álvaro Soler del Campo, "La Real Armería en el retrato español de corte," in *El arte del poder: la Real Armería y el retrato de corte*, ed. Álvaro Soler del Campo (Madrid: Museo Nacional del Prado, 2010), 55–87; Miguel Falomir, "El retrato de corte," in *El retrato del*

However, the image closest in form to the drawing is found in plate 117, which is part of the epic poem, *Theuerdank* (1517, printed around 1526) (Fig. 2). The woodcuts were designed by Hans Schaeufelein, Leonhard Beck, Hans Burgkmair, and others. The horse's analogous step, the knight in half armor's figure, the lance's presence, and the rider's rigid bodily posture constitutes the clearest precedent for our illustration in it. We must also mention some later images that could have been inspired by Beck's plate, such as the one illustrating Olivier de la Marche's *Le Chevalier Délibéré* (ca. 1553) (Fig. 3).

A similar one is repeated in the tapestry titled *The Review of the Troops in Barcelona*, from the series *The Conquest of Tunis* (1554) (Fig. 4), designed by Jan Cornelisz Vermeyen (painter) and Pieter Coecke (painter) van Aelst and woven by Willem Pannemaker.

The tapestry series was displayed during important ceremonies for the Habsburg lineage, so it is assumed that the author of the drawings could have seen them in Toledo, either during the wedding of Philip II and Isabella of Valois or the oath-taking of Prince Don Carlos (1560). However, as Checa points out, we should not forget that "between 1555 and 1560, Frans Hohenberg engraved a series of prints heavily inspired by Vermeyen's tapestries," thus, giving them wider dissemination.[22] The formal similarity between the image of Don Carlos and the Infante Dom Luís of Portugal, the figure in the foreground, is evident.[23] The most notable difference is found in the position of the spirited horse of the Portuguese, which has been replaced by a martial trot more akin to the representations of Beck, Burgkmair, or Titian. In any case, it is noticeable that the

---

Renacimiento, ed. Museo Nacional del Prado (Madrid: Ediciones El Viso, 2008), 109–24.

22 Checa Cremades, *Carlos V, a caballo*, 52.

23 According to Patrimonio Nacional, the owner of the tapestry, the character in the foreground is Infante Dom Luís, brother of Empress Isabel, great-uncle of Prince Don Carlos. However, Ian Buchanan supports a different opinion: "The horseman in the foreground to the right, who looks out of the tapestry, resembles known portraits of and statues of the Duke of Alba, Ferdinand Álvarez de Toledo (1507–82). The boy who rides behind him may be his five-years-old son García, who accompanied him in the expedition, or a page." Iain Buchanan, *Habsburg Tapestries* (Turnhout: Brepols Publishers, 2016), 190.

Figure 2. Leonhard Beck, (attributed), *Die geuerlicheiten vnd eins Teils der geschichten des loblichen streytparen vnd hochberümbten helds vnd Ritters herr Tewrdannckhs*, 1517, plate 117, woodcut, Nürnberg, Hannsen Schönsperger, R/5175. Image, under CC-BY license, from the collections of the National Library of Spain, Madrid.

anonymous artist based in Toledo was familiar with some of these images, which were part of the visual culture of erudite circles in the imperial city. However, we cannot affirm which images could be identified as his or her direct source.

Figure 3. Olivier La Marche, *El caballero determinado / traducido de lengua francesa en castellana por Hernando de Acuña*, fol. 99v, sixteenth century, manuscript, pen and ink drawing, 20 x 15 cm, MSS/1475. Image, under CC-BY license, from the collections of the National Library of Spain, Madrid.

The Enemies at the Horse's Feet

In *Theuerdank*'s plate 81 (Fig. 5), the knight appears with his enemy at the feet of his horse.

The same motif can be found in the series of engravings titled *The Victories of Charles V* with designs by Maarten van Heemskerck and published by Hieronymus Cock (1555–56). The engravings influenced numerous works due to the wide distribution of seven editions produced between 1556 and around 1640, contemporary with the writing of the *Relación de la christiana rogativa*. Among the total set of twelve engravings, special attention is warranted for plates II and V, which represent the *Battle of Pavia* (1525) (Fig. 6) and the *First Siege of Vienna* (1529) (Fig. 7).

Figure 4. Willem Pannemaker, Pieter Coecke van Aelst, Jan Cornelisz Vermeyen, *The Review of the Troops in Barcelona* from the series *The Conquest of Tunis*, 1548–1554, tapestry, gold, silver, silk, wool, 538 x 715.5 cm. Photograph: Mario Sedeño. Palacio Real de Madrid, Patrimonio Nacional, 10005908. Reproduction rights granted by Patrimonio Nacional, available by CC-BY license.

In both engravings, we can observe the presence of the defeated enemy—the French and the Turks—at the feet of the victorious Catholic horseman. This motif aligns perfectly with Angulo's intentions, as expressed in a gloss of the *Relación de la christiana rogativa*:

> Spero con el favor de Dios y de su alteza ver humillados a su gremio todos los enemigos de su fe y destruidas todas las Heregias del Lutero y de todos los demás infieles que aqui se ven caidos debaxo de sus pies pronosticando de si mesmo esta destruicion viendo el Príncipe con vida tan milagrosa, como lo dice el personaje de Martin Lutero por la letra que sta debaxo . . .[24]

---

24 Angulo, *Relación de la Christiana rogativa*, fol. 78v.

Figure 5. Leonhard Beck (attributed), *Die geuerlicheiten vnd eins Teils der geschichten des loblichen streytparen vnd hochberümbten helds vnd Ritters herr Tewrdannckhs*, 1517, plate 81, woodcut, Nürnberg, Hannsen Schönsperger, R/5175. Image, under CC-BY license, from the collections of the National Library of Spain, Madrid.

Figure 6. Maarten van Heemskerck (inventor), Dirck Volckertsz. Coornhert (engraver) & Hieronymus Cock (Publisher), *Battle of Pavia*, from the series *The Victories of Charles V*, 1556, plate II, etching and engraving, 158 x 232 mm, Antwerp, Mayson de Hieronymus Cock, ER/2966. Image, under CC-BY license, from the collections of the National Library of Spain, Madrid.

[They await, with the favor of God and His Highness, to see all the enemies of their faith humiliated, and all the heresies of Luther and other infidels destroyed, lying beneath their feet. They themselves prophesy this destruction, seeing the prince miraculously alive, as stated by the words written beneath the portrait of Martin Luther . . .]

The commentary refers to an ominous inscription prominently placed next to the father of the Reformation. It prophesies: *Nunc fient filii mei orphani, et uxor mea vidua* (Now my sons will be orphans, and my wife a widow).

Figure 7. Maarten van Heemskerck (inventor), Dirck Volckertsz. Coornhert (engraver) & Hieronymus Cock (Publisher), *First Siege of Vienna*, from the series *The Victories of Charles V*, 1556, plate V, etching and engraving, 158 x 232 mm, Antwerp, Mayson de Hieronymus Cock, ER/2966. Image, under CC-BY license, from the collections of the National Library of Spain, Madrid.

The Recovery of the Crusading Spirit of the *Miles Christianus*

In the manuscript drawing, Don Carlos marches triumphantly over the bodies of four clearly identified enemies. The first among them is Sergius, who served as the Patriarch of Constantinople from 610 to 638 AD and became entangled in the theological Monothelite controversy.[25] In the second position is Octoman, a reference to

---

25 For further information, see Richard A. Norris, Jr. (ed.), *The Christological Controversy* (Philadelphia, PA: Fortress Press, 1980); Agustine Casiday and Frederick Norris (eds.), *The Cambridge History of Christianity: Volume 2, Constantine to c.600* (Cambridge: Cambridge Univ. Press, 2007).

Suleiman the Magnificent or Suleiman I, the tenth Sultan of the Ottoman Empire, who reigned from 1520 to 1566. Additionally, the figures of Martin Luther and the Prophet Mohammed are represented. The selection of these four figures may appear somewhat strained, particularly due to Sergius's chronological remoteness. However, we believe their inclusion can be reasonably explained by two significant motives. Firstly, the allusion to the Monothelite heresy evokes the memory of a pivotal figure in Visigothic society and the Catholic Church, namely Julián de Toledo. This archbishop and theologian is renowned for his staunch adherence to the anti-Monothelite dogma, and his writings held considerable relevance during the proceedings of the XIV and XV Councils of Toledo.[26] The author establishes a connection between Visigothic Toledo and the Castilian Counter-Reformation era of the heir, integrating both events into a providential narrative.[27] Secondly, the choice of four enemies holds an additional biblical reference: the four horsemen of the Apocalypse (Rev. 6). Don Carlos rides triumphantly over these four ungodly individuals, serving as a parallel to the well-known woodcut by Albrecht Dürer (1498). It is as if the artist intends to present a counterpart to the German's famous depiction.[28]

The image and text point to the heretic, including the unbeliever, as the enemy to be defeated. The Monotheist heretic, the Turk, the Protestant, and the Muslim fall at the feet of the "very high and very powerful prince Don Carlos." After conquering Death, the prince's second chance prompts Faith to sing a song to celebrate the blessed prince to whom God has granted another life. This miraculous event must terrify his enemies, who witness the power of God and the protection of their faithful rulers:

---

26 José Madoz, "San Julián de Toledo," *Estudios eclesiásticos* 26 (1952): 39–69.

27 These initial verses of the sonnet, "If the great king Recaredo destroyed the tyrannical/malice of the Arians: Sisebuto triumphed over the Romans ..." (translation by the author) underscore the continuity between Carlos' enterprise and Visigothic exploits.

28 Albrecht Dürer, *The Four Horsemen*, 1498, woodcut, 393 x 293 mm., INC/1 ILUSTRACIONES, Biblioteca Nacional de España.

Gaudia deterrent aduersos pulchra salutis,
dant celeresque manus: hostis acerbe ruit.[29]

[The immense joy of your recovery will strike fear into your adversary, compelling them to hasten their surrender: the enemy succumbs mercilessly.]

"Faith" declares that if the heretics trembled before the hand of Emperor Carlos in his fierce endeavor, the same is expected to happen under the future reign of the prince. Our drawing seems to embrace a warlike vision reminiscent of the ideals of the Templar crusaders, as expressed by the theological virtue:

[Fe] la destrucción en ti de luteranos
espero Carlos yo muy mas ufana.[30]

[[Faith] I hope, Charles, with great pride,
that you will destroy the Lutherans.]

Such words align with the spirit of some chivalry books published in the early sixteenth century, where, in the words of Almudena Izquierdo, a vision of the "eschatological hero, savior of the religion in danger from pagan attack" is revived.[31] In the context of religious wars and the expansionist politics of the infidels, literature creates the figure of the "Catholic and virtuous" knight, who takes center stage in books such as *Las Sergas de Esplandián* by Garci Rodríguez de Montalvo (1510), *Florisando* by Páez de Ribera (1510), or *Lisuarte de Grecia* by Juan Díaz (1526), where, as explained by Izquierdo, the aim is to "shape a hero surrounded by an aura of a crusader knight who will enter the collective imagination through his struggle against the Muslims."[32] This crusading spirit is in line with the character of the *miles Christi* as a defender of the

---

29 Angulo, *Relación de la Christiana rogativa*, fol. 78v.
30 Ibid.
31 Almudena Izquierdo, "De los ensueños del pasado al *miles Christi*: ecos literarios en el prólogo de las Sergas de Esplandián," in *"En Doiro, Antr'o Porto e Gaia": Estudos de Literatura Medieval Ibérica*, ed. José Carlos Ribeiro Miranda Árbol and Rafaela da Câmara Silva (Porto: Estratégias Criativas, 2017), 564–65.
32 Ibid., 571.

religion, already described at the end of the thirteenth century in the *Book of the Order of Chivalry* by Ramon Llull. Additionally, the constant presence of warrior saints such as Saint George or Saint Michael, whose visual depiction resembles that of armed knights, should not be unrelated to this cultural movement.

The so-called "spiritual chivalry narratives," which are more characteristic of the mid-sixteenth century, align closely with the peaceful ideals associated with the Irenist assumptions derived from Erasmus of Rotterdam's *Enchiridion* and the spirit of the Peace of Augsburg (1555). However, the image of the armed knight, depicted as a defender of the true Faith and a member of the *Ecclesia militans*, seems to draw inspiration from the idealized warrior monk image popularized by Bernard of Clairvaux in the early twelfth century.

If the reception and interpretation of an image depend on the recipient's culture, it's crucial to explore social practices and cultural events in which people participate. This militaristic interpretation of the *miles Christi*, as opposed to the classical heroic one, can also be traced in other contexts.[33] For instance, in the triumphal processions led by Emperor Charles V, direct references to earthly, not spiritual, battles against the infidel are evident. Upon his entry into Milan in 1541, for instance, he was received with four triumphal arches designed by Giulio Romano, one of which depicted the equestrian figure of the Emperor triumphing over his adversaries— an Indian, an African, and a Turk.[34] Don Carlos, in the wake of his grandfather, is expected to assume a similar role, as seen in Alvar Gómez de Castro's account of the reception for Queen Elizabeth of Valois in Toledo and the dispatches related to the transfer of Saint Eugene's body by Antonio de Ribera:

> Si vosotros dos poderosísimos Reynos [Francia y España] conservays la presente concordia, el Turco será destruydo, los moros

---

33 For a discussion of triumphal entries where ephemeral art is conceived as a process of communication against the Other (Lutherans, Mohammed, heretics, etc.), see Borja Franco Llopis, "Imágenes de la herejía y de los protestantes en el arte efímero, de los Austrias," *Cahiers d'études des cultures ibériques et latino-américaines* 4 (2018): 39–64.

34 Giovanni Alberto Albicante, *Trattato del intrar in Milano di Carlo V C. sempre Aug. con le propie figura de li archi* (Milano: Andrea Calvo, 1541).

serán vuestros tributarios, la religión se limpiará de la mancha de
Luthero, y el mundo terna sossiego bienaventurado.[35]

[If you, two powerful Kingdoms [France and Spain], maintain
this present concord, the Turk will be defeated, the Moors will
become your tributaries, religion will be cleansed from the stain
of Luther, and the world will enjoy blessed peace.]

A Carlos, príncipe de la juventud a quien su padre Philippo consagra a la religión, y su abuelo Carlos V le incita a toda grandeza.
[El autor describe las iconografías] Tiene por ornamento una
mujer alegre con una flor. *Spes publica*. Esperanza pública. Otra
mujer temerosa. *Asia trepidas*. Asia temerosa.[36]

[To Charles, the prince of youth, whom his father Philip dedicates to religion, and his grandfather Charles V encourages to
all greatness. [The author describes the iconographies] He is
adorned with a joyful woman holding a flower. *Spes publica*. Public hope. Another fearful woman. *Asia trepidas*. Fearful Asia.]

There is evidence that the spiritual weapons described in the
Enchiridion played an undeniable role in the humanistic landscape
of the first decades of the sixteenth century. However, the visual
and literary culture found in chivalric literature, festivals, ephemeral architectures, and the military context of their production suggests that the audience was influenced by more immediate and
down-to-earth situations rather than the abstract battle between
virtues and vices, as proposed by Erasmus' followers. According to

---

35 Alvar Gómez de Castro, *Recebimiento que la Imperial ciudad de Toledo hizo a la Magestad de la Reyna nuestra señora doña Ysabel, hija del Rey Henrico II de Francia quando nueuuamente entro en ella a celebrar las fiestas de sus felicissemas bodas con el Rey don Philippe nuestro señor II deste nombre* (Toledo: Juan de Ayala, 1561), fol. 50v.

36 Antonio de Ribera, *Copilación de los despachos tocantes a la tra[n]slacio[n] del bendicto cuerpo de Sant Eugenio martyr primer Arçobispo de Toledo, hecha de la Abbadia de Sandonis en Francia a esta sancta Yglesia. Y la relacion del felicissimo viage que hizo el illustre y muy reuerendo señor don Pedro Manrique canonigo de la mesma sancta yglesia, por el dicho cuerpo sancto. Con el sole[n]nissimo rescibimiento que se hizo en esta ciudad de Toledo* (Toledo: Miguel Ferrer, 1566), f. 33r.

our understanding, we would make a contextual error if we solely regarded the *miles Christi* as a spiritual soldier.

Conclusion

The game of political favor was built upon the presentation of a gift and the construction of a powerful image of the future sovereign. Texts, images, and material culture converged in a field of relationships where each agent played their own game. Don Gastón de Peralta, 3rd Marquis of Falces, was finally appointed as the 3rd Viceroy of New Spain in 1566, although it is unclear if Don Carlos had a role in that decision. What seems evident is that the Marquis' gift was part of a strategy to defend his political interests, employing discourse that extolled the prince's virtues, alongside with prayers and ceremonies—*rogativas*—organized in the city ruled by the nobleman to thank God for his recovery, serving as a perfect excuse to bolster his own virtues.

The interpretation of this image of the *miles Christi* should not be confined merely to its iconographic significance, as the iconographic approach must consider the functioning of the visual corpus within the intricate courtly context. The manuscript book, a cultural artifact, presents an image that conveys a theological-political message produced within a specific material and visual culture associated with social practices such as gift-giving and festive celebrations.

In summary, an image of Don Carlos, constructed from the memory of his lineage, places the weak heir in the wake of his grandfather, the Emperor Charles V, attempting to legitimize his right to exercise power and heralding the arrival of a new defender of Catholic orthodoxy, as stated in the agreements of Chapter XXIII of the Order of the Golden Fleece (1559).[37] All of this benefited the astute marquis.

Universidad Nacional de Educación a Distancia

---

37 For further information, see Joaquín Azcárraga Servet, "Felipe II: el Toisón de Oro y los sucesos de Flandes," *Cuadernos de Historia del Derecho* 6 (1999): 475–78.

Inventing John Donne: Temptations of the Biographer

John N. Wall

A Cautionary Tale in Honour of the 400th Anniversary of the Consecration of Trinity Chapel at Lincoln's Inn on May 23rd, 1623, and Donne's Sermon preached on that Occasion

THE subject of this essay is the role of fiction in the biography of the priest and poet John Donne. Biography as a form is necessarily artificial. In the end, all biography is a form of fiction. Donne lends himself well to writers of biography because there is a great deal about his life that we do know, at least in comparison to the life of his slightly older contemporary William Shakespeare.[1] And, there is, of course, his work, much of which is occasion-specific, from his poems lamenting the death of Elizabeth Drury, the first of which was published in the year following her death in 1610, to his sermons preached on very specific occasions and in particular locations, and his *Devotions upon Emergent Occasions*, published in early 1624, only a few months after he experienced the illness that precipitated its composition.

Many biographies of Donne have appeared over the years, beginning with Isaak Walton's *Life of Donne* (1640), only nine years after Donne's death in 1631. But interest in Donne spurred by the early twentieth century's recovery of the metaphysical poets has led

---

1 R. C. Bald, the author of what is still, in my view, the best biography of Donne, claimed that "Donne must be the earliest major poet in English of whom an adequate biography is possible." In *John Donne: A Life* (Oxford, 1970), 1.

to a series of Donne biographies beginning in the later twentieth century. Basic to this list is R. C. Bald's magisterial *John Donne: A Life* of 1970, followed only a decade later by John Carey's *John Donne: Life, Mind, & Art* of 1981.[2] This momentum has continued in the twenty-first century, with David Colclough's *John Donne's Professional Lives* (Brewer, 2003) and John Stubbs' *John Donne: The Reformed Soul* (Norton, 2006). Yet the interest in Donne's life continues to grow, if the enthusiastic reception awarded the latest biography of Donne—Katherine Rundell's Super-*Infinite: The Transformations of John Donne* (Farrar Strauss & Giroux, 2022)—is any indication.[3]

The role of fiction in Rundell's biography will be the chief concern of this essay, but before getting to it, I want to consider briefly current understandings and best practices concerning the issue of what latitude a biographer has in reimagining the subject of a biography. On the one hand, I think we recognize that a responsible biographer is called upon to create a coherent narrative of an author's life, not simply to arrange the surviving data into a chronological list. We also recognize that in creating this narrative, a biographer must interpret the surviving data concerning the author's life, and that there are gaps in the data to be reckoned with, works by the author to be interpreted, and conclusions to be drawn.

Therefore, we must acknowledge, even biography, with its goal of telling the truth about an author's life, will contain what we must acknowledge as fiction. Biography therefore comes to reside within an artful but paradoxical conversation between the known and the imagined. Thus the critic Craig Brown is led to quote admiringly Peter Ackroyd to the effect that while "Fiction requires truth-telling . . . in a biography one can make things up." But Brown is also compelled to acknowledge the value of data; he says in the same essay that the biographer "is at the mercy of information," even though, he writes, "information is seldom there when you want it."[4] Therefore even Brown, while he affirms the reality that biography necessarily

---

2 Oxford, 1981.
3 Katherine Rundell, *Super-Infinite: The Transformations of John Donne* (New York, 2022).
4 Craig Brown, "Nothing Is Real: Craig Brown on the Slippery Art of Biography," https://lithub.com/nothing-is-real-craig-brown-on-

has a fictional dimension to it, also agrees with the biographer Mary Purcell, who in her essay "The Art of Biography" reminds us that the biographer "must discipline himself as a craftsman; he has to control his imagination for he may not stray beyond the limits the factual evidence at his disposal imposes upon him; his skill at his craft will show in the selection and interpretation of his material."[5] Or, as Natalie Zemon Davis put it in her reconstruction of the life of Martin Guerre, what the biographer offers is "in part invention, but held tightly in check by the voices of the past."[6]

Brown, Purcell, and Davis agree that when we are dealing with what Brown calls "the slippery art of biography," we must recognize both the inevitability and the limits of fiction's role. With that as background, we turn to Katherine Rundell's new (and prize-winning[7] and highly lauded by the early reviewers) biography of John Donne. Rundell begins *Super-Infinite: The Transformations of John Donne*, by asserting the claim[8] that the "power of John Donne's words nearly killed a man."[9] This dramatic event took place, according to Rundell, in the "late spring of 1623, on the morning of Ascension Day," when Donne "had finally secured for himself celebrity, fortune and a captive audience." "[H]is preaching was famous across the whole of London," Rundell tells us, and, as a result, "Word went out: wherever he was, people came flocking, often in their thousands, to hear him speak."

This day, according to Rundell, Donne preached at Lincoln's Inn, "where a new chapel was being consecrated." The way Rundell states these two facts, oddly, makes no connection between Donne's preaching and the chapel's consecration service. In her account, it is as though Donne woke up that morning in the Deanery at St Paul's, made a decision to take the "fifteen minutes' easy walk across London," and decided to preach. Still, she says, on a day when a

---

the-slippery-art-of-biography/. This talk was delivered at the 2019 Edinburgh International Book Festival.

5   Mary Purcell, "The Art of Biography," *Studies: An Irish Quarterly Review* 48, no. 191 (1959): 305–17.
6   In *The Return of Martin Guerre* (Cambridge, 1983).
7   It was awarded the Baillie Gifford Prize for Non-Fiction in 2022.
8   A claim previously unmentioned among Donne biographers.
9   Rundell, *Super-Infinite*, 1.

chapel consecration was going on, people "came flocking." As she tells it, this sermon must have been delivered outside this chapel, since, as we will see, Trinity Chapel had pews, and, Rundell tells us, while Donne was preaching his sermon, the crowd "pushed closer to hear his words," a move difficult to make when people are seated in pews.[10]

As a result, Rundell says, "men in the crowd were shoved to the ground and trampled." Note well, "to the ground," not to the floor, yet another indication that Rundell imagines Donne's sermon taking place outside the Chapel, or at least separate from the consecration service for the chapel. Yet, she goes on, doubling down on her claim that when "Two or three were endangered, and taken up for dead," it was during Donne's sermon. But, she assures us, "There's no record of Donne halting his sermon; so it's likely that he kept going in his rich, authoritative voice as the bruised men were carried off and out of sight."[11]

This opening scene, so vividly realized by Rundell, even though it is only two pages long, is sufficiently dramatic and compelling to have caught the special attention of several of the laudatory reviews of Rundell's work. Adam Kirsch, in the *New Yorker*, interprets Rundell's account to mean that the crowd's "press and thronging . . . led to a stampede."[12] Rowan Williams, in the *New Statesman*, begins his review by noting that while the "last thing that keeps contemporary Anglican preachers awake at night is the risk of serious injury resulting from the crush of people in their congregations," but Williams asserts, "Rundell reminds us . . . the risk was real enough when John Donne was in the pulpit."[13] Catherine Nicholson, in her *London Review of Books* review, makes the most of Rundell's claims: describing how "Rundell conjures the scene on a Sunday morning in April 1623, when Donne 'delivered a guest sermon in the new chapel at

---

10 For a detailed reconstruction of Trinity Chapel at Lincoln's Inn on the day of its consecration, see The Virtual Trinity Chapel Project website (https://vtcp.chass.ncsu.edu/).

11 Rundell, *Super-Infinite*, 1.

12 https://www.newyorker.com/magazine/2022/10/10/john-donnes-proto-modernism.

13 https://www.newstatesman.com/culture/books/2023/02/super-infinite-review-katherine-rundell-john-donne-biography.

Lincoln's Inn.'" Nicholson elaborates dramatically on Rundell's own dramatic elaboration:

> The chapel building filled, and over-filled, with what a contemporary report described as "a great concourse of noblemen and gentlemen." As the crowd pressed forward to hear Donne speak, the situation grew dangerous; in the "extreme press and throng," men stumbled and fell, or perhaps they simply couldn't breathe: "Two or three were endangered and taken up for dead at the time." As Rundell observes, "there's no record of Donne halting his sermon; so it's likely that he kept going in his rich, authoritative voice as the bruised men were carried off and out of sight."[14]

There is, indeed, no record of Donne's halting his sermon.[15] Nor, as we will see, is there any record of Donne's being interrupted during his sermon, nor that anyone was shoved to the ground (or the floor) during his sermon, or that the crowd present on that occasion came expressly to hear Donne, or, in fact, that any of the events of that May 22, 1623, unfolded in the way Rundell describes them, or that most of them ever happened at all. Unfortunately for Rundell's approach to writing Donne's biography, the one occasion in John Donne's life for which there is a remarkably abundant supply of data happens to be about his role in the events of the morning of Thursday, May 22, the Feast of the Ascension in 1623, at Lincoln's Inn. May 22 in 1623 was the date chosen by the Inn for

---

14 https://www.lrb.co.uk/the-paper/v45/n02/catherine-nicholson/batter-my-heart. Nicholson is apparently unaware that worship services take place in the Church of England on days of the week other than Sundays, and certainly unaware that the consecration of Trinity Chapel took place on the Feast of the Ascension in May of 1623, a feast that is always forty days after Easter Day, thus is always on a Thursday in May, not ever a Sunday in April. Nicholson also thinks that Donne did not publish any of his poetry, a claim that would certainly surprise the Drury family.

15 A few years ago, working with Guy Holborn, the former Archivist at Lincoln's Inn, I pulled together a number of documents relating to this sermon, and the service that included it, onto a website (https://vtcp.chass.ncsu.edu/). Based on those materials, I've been wanting to tell someone my frustration about Rundell's account of Donne's sermon at Trinity Chapel.

the consecration of its newly-constructed Trinity Chapel, opening it officially for use as a worship space by the members of the Inn.

Four reports detailing this worship service and its setting in time and space have survived. They include two lengthy and detailed accounts now preserved in the Archives of Lincoln's Inn. One of these was written by a Fellow of Lincoln's Inn;[16] the other, bearing his official seal, is Bishop Montaigne's official account of his actions in consecrating the Chapel.[17] In addition to these two extensive accounts we also have two brief summaries of the day's events;[18] one (also written by a member of Lincoln's Inn) is now in the possession of the Society of Antiquaries, dated "Assencion Day 1623," and the other is one of John Chamberlain's letters to Sir Dudley Carleton, dated a week later, on May 30, 1623.[19] When taken together, these four documents provide us with a detailed, almost moment-by-moment description of the Service of Consecration for Trinity Chapel that did take place on May 22, Ascension Day, in 1623.[20]

All four of these documents are in essential agreement about what took place on that morning in late May at Lincoln's Inn. The two longest accounts give us the fullest amount of detail. To summarize what they tell us—this service, led by George Montaigne, the recently consecrated Bishop of London, lasted from 8:00 AM until 11:00 AM on the morning of May 23, 1623. The service started outside the Chapel, on the landing in front of the doorway to the Chapel, where a crowd had gathered, assembled on the ground in front of the Chapel.

Rundell's description of the events at Trinity Chapel on Ascension Day is of course dependent on her belief that the number of attendees at the Consecration ceremony was both large and

---

16 Lincoln's Inn, Ms. Archives ref J1 A2.
17 Lincoln's Inn, Ms. Archives ref J1 A1.
18 Society of Antiquaries MS 201 No. 37.
19 John Chamberlain, *Letters,* ed. Norman Egbert (Philadelphia: American Philosophical Society, 1939), II, 135.
20 All these documents, along with models of the outside and inside of Trinity Chapel on the day of its consecration, a recreation of the script for the full worship service, Donne's sermon, and a discussion of the Chapel's construction, are available on the website of the Virtual Trinity Chapel Project (https://vtcp.chass.ncsu.edu/), and have been for several years.

boisterous. But the only direct comment in any of these accounts about the size of the crowd is found in the anonymous account of the Consecration now in the archives of the Society of Antiquaries. To this observer there was a "Concourse & Confluence of people," but he goes on to say that it was smaller than in should have been, since "The Kings Councell vppon especiall Command sate that Day att white Hall, soe that only ye Bishop of London two Iudges & foure sergeants were ye men of (quality) that were present att ye Consecration."[21]

Furthermore, those in attendance were not random Londoners who "came flocking" to hear Donne preach, but were—in addition to a few members of the Royal Court[22]—chiefly members of England's legal community—Justices of England's highest courts, lawyers, members of Lincoln's Inn, and law students aspiring to become barristers, people described repeatedly in these documents as "worshipful and venerable men," men accustomed to behaving "decently and in good order." These were definitely not the kind of folks Rundell imagines as having "flocked" to hear Donne preach, pushing and shoving to get closer to him.

We are then told that[23]

> the reverend father in Christ [George Montaigne, Bishop of London], accompanied by many reverend and venerable men, approached the doorway of the chapel to be consecrated, and to him the venerable men Thomas Spenser, Richard Digges, and Egidius Tooker, esquires, ... and William Ravenscroft, one of the worshipful counselors of the aforementioned Inn, indicated that they had ... seen to the erection and equipment of the said chapel, on their own private grounds and with their own private funds. And they yielded their rights in the same, and so ... they granted, gave, and donated the aforesaid chapel to God almighty and to the highest, holy, and indivisible Trinity, and ... they presented and handed over the keys of the aforesaid chapel to

---

21 For the full text of this document, see https://vtcp.chass.ncsu.edu/society-of-antiquaries/.

22 Including the Earl of Southampton, Shakespeare's former patron.

23 The quote printed here is taken from the description of the service provided by a Member of the Inn. The account provided by Bishop Montaigne agrees with it in every detail.

the same reverend, humbly beseeching the said reverend father to declare and consecrate the aforesaid chapel to the everlasting honor and service of God almighty, and the use of those staying in the aforesaid Inn.[24]

Bishop Montaigne and Thomas Wilson, his chaplain, then entered the building, offered prayers, then turned to "the congregation still standing at the doors of the chapel" and read a lengthy statement which the Inn's Fellow claims formed the actual moment of consecration. Only then was "the whole congregation … called together into the chapel."[25]

What followed on that day, once everyone was in the Chapel, was the sequence of services prescribed for Sundays and Holy Days, like the Feast of the Ascension in parishes, collegiate churches, and cathedrals across England—Morning Prayer, with its readings set by the Prayer Book's lectionary, followed by the Great Litany and Holy Communion, with a sermon, a sequence of events that filled the three-hour span between 8:00 AM and 11:00 AM.[26] In this service, Donne's sermon followed the Great Litany rather than coming after recitation of the Nicene Creed in the Communion Service, but otherwise the service was what was provided for, prescribed for use, and scripted by the Book of Common Prayer. Afterwards, Bishop Montaigne tells us, he went downstairs to consecrate the building's undercroft for use as a burial ground for Fellows of Lincoln's Inn. When the service was over, some three hours after it began, everyone retired to the Inn's ancient Great Hall, directly adjacent to the new Chapel, for a festive reception.

---

24 The Latin text and a translation of this document are available on the Virtual Trinity Chapel website (https://vtcp.chass.ncsu.edu/) and also in *Anglican & Episcopal History* 81 (2012): 148–99.

25 Our measurements of the Chapel indicate that it provided in 1623 seating for about 250 people, with standing room at the back for perhaps another 25 or 30.

26 For a recreation of these services, pulling together the liturgical texts from the Book of Common Prayer (1604) with the special prayers and readings specified by the several accounts of these services, see the Virtual Trinity Chapel website (https://vtcp.chass.ncsu.edu/the-script-for-the-service/).

And so we leave them, at least for the moment, celebrating the accomplishment of the Fellows of Lincoln's Inn in raising the money and seeing through to completion and consecration of Trinity Chapel. For us, however, the most important point to note here is that, unlike Rundell's account, we now know that Donne's sermon was not a stand-alone event that happened to take place on the day Trinity Chapel was consecrated, but an integral part of that larger service. We also need to recognize that nowhere in either the Fellow's account or Bishop Montaigne's account of events—the two longest and most detailed of all these accounts—is there any mention of the "Two or three [who] were endangered, and taken up for dead." Nor do any of our contemporary witnesses report that the congregation was unruly, or that Donne's sermon was interrupted, or that anyone rushed forward to get closer to him.

One is therefore left with the conundrum of understanding where Rundell found data or inspiration from which to extrapolate, or, perhaps better put, to fabricate, her account of this ceremony. The answer—to the extent there is an answer—lies in the other two of our sources: the anonymous account now in the possession of the Society of Antiquaries, which was written by a member of Lincoln's Inn on Ascension Day itself; and the letter John Chamberlain wrote to Sir Dudley Carleton a week later. The Society of Antiquaries document, written on the day of the event, brings us closest to what actually happened. Our anonymous author says:

> Vppon Thursday beinge Assention Day was ye Chappel of Lincolnes Inne Consecrated, where there was such a Concourse & Confluence of people that Sr Francis Lee was soe thronged that hee fell downe deade in ye presse, And was Caryed away into a Gentlemans Chamber & wth much a doe Recouered.[27]

So, we now have an eyewitness account of the Consecration which includes a description of the crowd's behavior as "a Concourse & Confluence of people," although we must note this account does not describe the crowd as pushing and shoving. According to this

---

27 Society of Antiquaries MS 201 No. 37: Account of the Consecration of the chapel of Lincoln's Inn, by George Montaigne, Bp of London, Ascension Day, 1623. Transcription by Dr. Steven May, Emory University, found here: https://vtcp.chass.ncsu.edu/society-of-antiquarie.

account, the number of people who reacted adversely to the behavior of the crowd is down to one. So we learn that one person fainted—in the terminology of the day, he "fell downe dead in the presse"—and we have his name—Sir Francis Lee—and we know the author of this account believed that Sir Francis Lee fell because he was "soe thronged" by the crowd.

This narrator then moves on, chronologically, to describe what happened next; his account replicates, albeit more succinctly, the account given by the Fellow of Lincoln's Inn in his account. "The manner of itt [i.e., of the Consecration Service] was in this Manner. / First ye Bishop himselfe alone wth Wilson his Chaplayne entredd ye Chauncell." Then we get a description of the prayers Bishop Montaigne prayed, and things he did, repeating information we find in the Inn's Fellow's account. Eventually we are told, "This beeinge done ye Mynister beganne Devine service & reade ye 24.27 & 28 psalmes, And for ye Chapters ye i of Kinges 8. & Iohn ye 10th, And then ye Letanye & soe to ye Sermon, where Doctor Doone preached & tooke or his Text a scripture out of Iohn."

Folks familiar with the Church of England's Book of Common Prayer will recognize that "Divine Service" means the Office of Morning Prayer, which consists of Prayers, Anthems, Versicles and Responses, readings from the Book of Psalms (on this day Psalms 24, 27, and 28), a full chapter from the Old Testament and another from the New Testament—at least forty-five minutes of reading—followed by the Great Litany, with its extended set of prayers (at least another half an hour), and only then do we get to "the Sermon, where Doctor Donne preached." Furthermore, the service was not over when Donne finished his sermon; instead it went on for another hour, completing the sequence of Prayer Book worship on Holy Days with a service of Holy Communion.

And, nowhere, in this detailed account by an eyewitness, from its opening comments about Bishop Montaigne's actions at Trinity Chapel's doorway through its list of the Order of Service, and its comments on Donne's sermon, is there any further mention of the fate of Sir Francis Lee. It is very clear from the sequence of events contained in this account that Lee's collapse must have taken place before the Consecration service, when the congregation was first gathering in the Chapel's churchyard and crowding around the steps up to the landing outside the Chapel's door, while awaiting the appearance of Bishop Montaigne, at 8:00 AM, and not, as Rundell argues, at least an hour and a quarter later, after the crowd had entered the building and dispersed itself among the Chapel's array of seating and standing room.

Then, this writer goes on to describe the Consecration service itself as having proceeded exactly as our other sources describe it, again with no mention at all that Sir Francis Lee passed out during the service itself or that the service—or Donne's sermon—were interrupted in any way. So, we may infer that the behavior of the crowd of judges, lawyers, and members of the nobility that might have caused Sir Francis Lee to pass out took place outside Trinity Chapel, while the crowd was assembling and awaiting the arrival of Bishop Montaigne and his entourage so the service could begin.

Or, perhaps, Sir Francis' collapse could have happened when the congregation was invited by Bishop Montaigne to enter the building after he had offered his prayers inside. But I personally am betting on the gathering time—these folks knew how to process in an orderly fashion and probably did as they filed into the Chapel. Supporting this argument is the fact that the seating area inside the Chapel was divided into sections and assigned to different categories of members of Lincoln's Inn—one area allocated to senior members, another area to the broader membership, and yet another area to those preparing for entry into the legal profession. So the majority of those waiting to process into Trinity Chapel would have known where they were headed and would have organized themselves accordingly, knowing that their assigned seats were waiting for them.[28]

Only when we turn to the letter John Chamberlain wrote to his friend in the Hague on May 30, a week after the Consecration ceremony at Trinity Chapel, do we find the original source for Rundell's

---

28 There are a number of reasons why Sir Francis Lee fainted on this occasion, the effects of being in a closely-packed crowd (the "Concourse & Confluence of people") being only one of them. The website WebMD (https://www.webmd.com/) includes getting overheated in a crowded space as one cause of fainting, but the average high temperature in London in late May and early June is usually only in the high 60s and low 70s. It is more likely that Sir Francis was experiencing low blood sugar, dehydration, low blood pressure, heart arrhythmia, or other heart problems.

quotations about these events and the starting point for her speculations. In his letters to Sir Dudley Carleton, Chamberlain consistently seeks to keep his friend informed about events in London and especially in Court, as well as about the topics of conversation among their friends. Following his usual pattern, Chamberlain's letter of May 30, 1623, includes lots of court news, especially concerning the state of King James' efforts to achieve the Spanish Match for his son Charles. At this point in that long narrative of frustration, Chamberlain expects that the negotiations are going well, and that "We look daily to heare of the solemnization of the marriage."[29] As part of those preparations, Chamberlain notes that a week ago "the Spanish ambassador laide the foundation or first stone of the chappell that is to be built at St. James for the Infanta."[30]

Then, almost as an aside, or perhaps as a contrast to the construction of a chapel intended for Roman Catholic worship, Chamberlain says, of a chapel intended for worship according to the Book of Common Prayer,

> Lincolns Ynne new chappell was consecrated with more solemnitie by the bishop of London on Ascension day, where there was great concourse of noblemen and gentlemen wherof two or three were indaungered and taken up dead for the time with the extreme presse and thronging.

In Chamberlain's account of the events of Ascension Day at Trinity Chapel, the story told by the anonymous member of Lincoln's Inn goes through some subtle but nevertheless significant changes. The anonymous writer's description of "Concourse & Confluence" has become an "extreme presse and thronging" and the unfortunate Sir Francis Lee has become "two or three [who] were indaungered and taken up dead." Chamberlain then goes on immediately to say that "The Deane of Paules made an excellent sermon (they say) concerning dedications." Thus in Chamberlain's account, unlike all the other accounts of the events at Trinity Chapel, there is no mention of the hours of worship services that preceded and followed Donne's

---

29 In *Anglican & Episcopal History* 81 (2012): 207–10.

30 This Chapel, now known as the Queen's Chapel, was controversial because it was to be the first place in which the Mass was to be celebrated legally in England since the Elizabethan Settlement of Religion in 1559.

sermon. But Chamberlain's insertion of the words "they say" shows us that he was actually not there, that his account of events was dependent on hearsay evidence. So, Chamberlain's version, based on other people's accounts, suggests that in the days after the Feast of the Ascension, the story both lost some aspects of the story but also grew in detail in some of its specifics, as stories passed through oral transmission are often likely to do.

Rundell's overall account of Donne's activities on Ascension Day in 1623, plus her use of Chamberlain's language and tone and her direct quotes—especially her use of Chamberlain's phrase "Two or three were endangered, and taken up for dead"[31]—make clear that Chamberlain's letter to Sir Dudley Carleton is her source for what Donne was about at Lincoln's Inn on the Feast of the Ascension in 1623.[32] What Rundell has done is to continue the process of elaborating on the events of May 23 1623, begun by John Chamberlain when he expanded the number of gentlemen who collapsed while the crowd waited to be admitted to the Chapel from one (Sir Francis Lee) to "two or three," a process continued by Adam Kirsch, in his *New Yorker* review when he interprets Rundell's account that "men in the crowd were shoved to the ground and trampled" to mean that the crowd's "press and thronging ... led to a stampede."

In spite of Rundell's belief that the consecration of Trinity Chapel was yet another opportunity for Donne to dazzle the congregation with his preaching style, all accounts of the service make clear that the reason for the gathering of a congregation at Trinity Chapel was for the Consecration ceremony. Donne, then Dean of St Paul's, was chosen as preacher for the occasion not because he was a celebrity preacher, as Rundell claims, but because he had been involved in the process of planning and constructing Trinity Chapel from the beginning. Donne had served as the official Preacher for Lincoln's Inn from 1616 until his appointment as Dean of St Paul's in 1621. He had supported plans to build the Chapel, had preached at least one sermon encouraging the Inn to undertake its construction, been instrumental in raising funds to support the project, and had laid the cornerstone for construction of the building. He contributed

---

31 Without attributing her source for her direct borrowing to Chamberlain.
32 Indeed, it is likely to have been her only source.

his own funds to the construction, a gift marked by a part of the program of stained glass, which, loosely translated, reads, "I, John Donne, Dean of St Paul's, caused this to be made."

In fact, far from being a sermon that would enhance Donne's reputation as a preacher for a wide general audience, Donne's sermon is very much about the chapel itself, and very much directed very personally to his former colleagues at the Inn. He starts by reminding them of how little money they had for the project at its beginning, and what a significant accomplishment it was that it is now complete and being put into service. His sermon is about what makes a building holy, which turns out to be the worship that takes place within it, the very worship that they are all involved in at that moment, and the members of the congregation who gather inside it to take part in that worship:

> This Festivall belongs to us, because it is the consecration of that place, which is ours ... But it is more properly our Festivall, because it is the consecration of our selves to *Gods* service.... Your *Bodies* are holy, by the inhabitation of those sanctified *Soules* ... These walles are holy, because the *Saints* of *God* meet here ... But yet these places are not onely consecrated and sanctified by your comming; but to bee sanctified also for your coming; that so, as the Congregation sanctifies the place, the place may sanctifie the Congregation, too.[33]

As our anonymous reporter of the event describes it, Donne's point is that it is the use of the Chapel in "prayer preachinge Administration of ye Sacrament of ye Bodye & blood of Christ, And singinge of Hymnes & psalms" that really consecrates a place of worship. But the worship by the congregation in this space is not an end in itself but a consecration of the worshippers to God's service. Interestingly, our anonymous writer thought Donne's sermon showed "superficiem but not Medullam Theologiae haveinge Eloqentiae satis but sapientiae parum"—that is, it showed the surface rather than the marrow of theology, having sufficient eloquence but little wisdom. So much for Rundell's claims about Donne's having a universally positive reputation as a great preacher!

---

33 From *The Sermons of John Donne*, ed. George Potter and Evelyn Simpson (Berkeley, 1959), IV, 364.

My point is, the crowd came to Trinity Chapel because it was a new church building (a rare thing in early seventeenth-century England), because many of those present had contributed to its construction, and because it was at Lincoln's Inn, an important part of the London legal and courtly worlds. Donne was the preacher because he had been involved in the construction of Trinity Chapel from the beginning and because he was the hometown boy who had made good by becoming Dean of St Paul's Cathedral. Thus, his sermon was not about demonstrating the glories of his preaching skill or satisfying a devoted audience who followed him wherever he preached, but about the occasion, about the act of consecration, about how the worship being done in that place and time by the people who showed up for that service functioned as consecration, setting Trinity Chapel apart from a secular to a holy purpose.

The historian Lewis Namier comments on the work of historians and on the temptations they face. "One would expect people to remember the past and imagine the future," he writes. "But in fact, when discoursing or writing about history, they imagine it in terms of their own experience ... they imagine the past and remember the future."[34] Donne surely would have been unhappy with Rundell's treatment; the past she imagines for him in her biography sets him apart from his community, makes his distinctiveness as a person about his showing off, praising him for what she sees as achieving personal gain and cultural prominence. Donne, in his sermon for Ascension Day in 1623, was about giving meaning to the occasion and giving thanks for what the Lincoln's Inn community had achieved, about understanding how the building they were inside of was both fulfillment of their aspirations and challenge to make good on the building's promise to enrich the life of the community and to further the larger goals of Christian living. One hopes Sir Francis Lee recovered from his collapse quickly enough to hear it.

North Carolina State University

---

34 Quoted in Craig Brown, "Nothing is Real: Craig Brown on the Slippery Art of Biography." https://lithub.com/nothing-is-real-craig-brown-on-the-slippery-art-of-biography/.

Printed and bound by CPI Group (UK) Ltd, Croydon, CR0 4YY
02/12/2024
14603683-0002